AF065168

CANADA'S MOST WANTED

Lisa Wojna

QUAGMIRE
PRESS

© 2010 by Quagmire Press Ltd.
First printed in 2010 10 9 8 7 6 5 4 3 2 1
Printed in Canada

All rights reserved. No part of this work covered by the copyrights hereon may be reproduced or used in any form or by any means—graphic, electronic or mechanical—without the prior written permission of the publisher, except for reviewers, who may quote brief passages. Any request for photocopying, recording, taping or storage on information retrieval systems of any part of this work shall be directed in writing to the publisher.

The Publisher: Quagmire Press Ltd.
Website: www.quagmirepress.com

Library and Archives Canada Cataloguing in Publication

Wojna, Lisa, 1962–
Canada's most wanted / Lisa Wojna.

Includes bibliographical references.
ISBN 978-1-926695-13-6

1. Fugitives from justice—Canada. 2. Criminals—Canada—Biography. I. Title.

HV6805.W65 2010   364.1092'271   C2010-904309-X

Project Director: Hank Boer
Project Editor: Kathy van Denderen
Cover Image: © Denis Jr. Tangney / iStockphoto

We acknowledge the support of the Alberta Foundation for the Arts for our publishing program.

PC: 1

Contents

INTRODUCTION **8**

STILL WANTED   **14**

    MIDSUMMER MASSACRE: **KEVIN VERMETTE** 17

    THE NEPHEW BANDIT: **RICHARD EARL RUPERT** 29

    A SHOT IN THE DARK: **RONALD JEFFREY BAX**............. 47

    "MAN OF GOD" TOO GOOD TO BE TRUE:
    FRED SIEBOLT HOFMAN 56

CASE CLOSED   **76**

    MACHINE GUN MOLLY: **MONIQUE PROIETTI** 78

    COVER GIRL BANDIT: **CHRISTINE BARTLETT**............... 89

    THE GENTLEMAN BANDIT: **EDWIN ALONZO BOYD** 99

    GONE FISHING: **TYSON CONN** 117

    MIRAMICHI MENACE: **ALLAN LEGERE**..................... 131

    AT ALL COSTS: **JAMES CHARLES KOPP** 140

    CHILDHOOD HORROR: **RICHARD STEVE GOLDBERG**........ 155

    TWISTED LOVE: **ALLAN DWAYNE SCHOENBORN** 161

HISTORICAL CASES   **188**

    RAT RIVER RECLUSE STILL ELUDES AUTHORITIES,
    EVEN AFTER DEATH: **ALBERT JOHNSON**................... 190

    PAINTED BLACK: **THE DONNELLY FAMILY** 223

NOTES ON SOURCES **253**

Dedication

This book is dedicated to those who thought they had a reason to turn to a life of crime or who spent some time on the wrong side of the law but were liberated from their circumstances through the power of choice.

Acknowledgements

I've said it before, but it must be said again—putting together an assortment of words that flow together to tell a story or a collection of stories that your publisher believes is worthy enough to make into a book is certainly not a solitary venture, though it might feel like one at times.

With that in mind, I'd like to thank every newshound, writer, broadcaster, observer, blogger, interpreter and columnist who has ever chronicled about the stories in this compilation. By upholding the age-old creed that "the public has the right to know," these many writers and their contributions, whether they appeared in the pages of a publication, legal documents or personal blogs, have to a great extent laid the groundwork for what appears in this book. When the secondary sources conflicted in thin details, I've tried to include these differences in the hope of providing readers with as much information as possible.

At the same time, the numerous weeks of perusing online archives, reading and re-reading countless newspaper articles, dissecting legal documents or court transcripts and trying to digest and rework all that information into some kind of new, exciting, cohesive package requires a great editor every bit as much as it needs a committed writer. My meagre efforts in adding to the public's right to know would have been significantly less successful without my gifted editor for this project, Kathy van Denderen. Thank you for your commitment and your patience.

Thank you to Linda and Darcy Benderski, proprietors of Rainbow Falls Resort in White Lake, Manitoba. Their generous donation of Internet time meant that I could work on this project in the middle of the Manitoba wilderness, which, in turn allowed my little girl to "4-3-2-1, cannonball!" off her auntie's dock all summer long.

Thank you to the staff at Wetaskiwin Public Library. As always, they graciously took the time to answer my many questions and requests.

Thank you to Faye, my long-time mentor who I am also privileged to call my friend. I also owe a debt of gratitude to Quagmire Press and its ongoing support of my projects. Thank you to my family—without each and every one of you all, this and anything else I do would be meaningless.

And thank you to Diana MacLeod, fellow writer and dear friend. Serendipity dictated that the two of us spoke on a day when I was particularly frustrated over not finding the appropriate "most wanted woman" to include in this book—Canada has its share of most wanted females, but these women are often one-time offenders or commit crimes and disappear, leaving sketchy bits of news behind and little for investigators to work with. Diana pointed me in the direction of Machine Gun Molly—a woman who, despite her criminal acts, captured the imagination of a nation and demonstrated how circumstances often affect behaviour. Her exploits can never be overlooked, but you cannot help but wonder that had she lived under different conditions, she might have put her impressive talents to better use—something that also could be said of many of the individuals profiled in this book.

Introduction

In North American society, our perspective of a fugitive from justice is somewhat coloured by images from Hollywood movies and the familiar black-and-white wanted posters popularized in tales of the Wild West. There's a kind of macabre glam to the likes of criminals such as Bonnie and Clyde, for example. Bonnie, attracted to the suave, easy-talking bad boy Clyde; Clyde, hopelessly in love with Bonnie from the time he first laid eyes on her. They were both just kids, really. What did they know? We recall our own foolish youth, and we sympathize with the characters. Even when we know the final chapter in that story, it's hard not to hope that maybe this version has a happy ending. Maybe, just maybe, they would find religion, change their wanton ways and go on to live a good life. At least, that's the way a movie is supposed to end, isn't it?

Here in Canada, moviemakers aren't as apt to glamorize our criminals in the same way. In fact, residents in one corner of the country aren't always aware of large-scale crooks whose activities are no less appalling than their U.S. counterparts and the news that these fugitives generate thousands of kilometres away. It's only when we uncover a Robert Pickton and learn of the horrendous acts of depravity and violence he committed on some of the most vulnerable members of our society that news of this kind travels the breadth of this large country.

That said, Canadians have been exposed to the wild and crazed antics of some of our more off-the-wall fugitives who, despite their foray on the wrong side of the law, somehow touch a soft spot in our hearts. Career criminals like Edwin Alonzo Boyd, a character many referred to during his tenure and in later years as the "gentleman bandit," made a name for himself as a prolific and somewhat successful bank robber. In reality, Boyd was more of a bungler than he was a big shot. It was his killer good looks, his suave demeanour and the flashy way he tossed himself over a bank counter and instructed the tellers to unload their drawers that strangely resonated in people's memories. It was like being caught up in the middle of a Hollywood drama. Only this wasn't Hollywood. This was a polite, unobtrusive, middle-income neighbourhood bank in Canada.

Boyd's exploits were short-lived; at least as far as bank robbery was concerned. He continued to entertain Canadians and dismay prison workers with repeated escapes and recaptures. Curious writers eventually penned two books about Boyd and his gang, and stories about the felons appear in several nonfiction compilations. And in 2005 the CBC released a documentary on the man and his cohorts.

Because Boyd had a reputation of talking tough but never hurting his victims, the title of "gentleman bandit" stuck.

But it was a misnomer, really. During his robberies, Boyd was involved in armed altercations with the police. And later on in life he exposed an even more deadly side to his personality. At the same time, we learn about some of his more redeeming qualities, such as caring for his wife and a friend after he was released from prison; both women struggled with physical and mobility challenges.

Stories like those of Boyd and of Bonnie and Clyde made headlines during their time and were depicted on the silver screen. True to Canadian form, the Boyd Gang was represented in a more low-key, nonfiction format, but the 2005 documentary produced similar results to a big screen movie in that the Canadian public was treated to an indepth understanding of the robbers.

These tales, and others like them, aren't depicting imaginary characters. During their four years together, Bonnie and Clyde and their gang robbed banks, stores and gas stations, used a variety of weapons to threaten their victims and even committed murder. That wasn't Hollywood; that was real life. When Boyd and his partners held up a local bank, it affected everyone in the neighbourhood. The knowledge that a complete stranger could target people in the perceived safety of their own community was terrifying.

Reading about the escapades of criminals like Bonnie and Clyde, or the members of the Boyd Gang, is solid proof of the adage that truth really is stranger than fiction. Events such

Introduction

as the ones described in their stories really happen, and they can happen to us. Perhaps that is at least part of the reason for the increasing popularity of true crime as a genre; there are people in our midst capable of grave and heinous acts. It's a fact that both intrigues and paralyzes us with fear. We are mystified about what catapults a person into a life of crime. We're appalled to think that we, or someone we love, could become a victim. And at the same time, we might find ourselves strangely compelled to feel sorry for a criminal when we learn about the struggles of his or her early life.

Accounts like these also serve as a window into the lives of the people who commit their energies to guarding the public's safety. The events that our peace officers have to deal with daily would be almost impossible to imagine were it not for the occasional foray into the criminal mind via evening newscasts, prime-time serials and reality television. Those glimpses make us ask ourselves how many crime scenes do police officers have to process during their careers? Do the images of mangled bodies or the stories of abuse they routinely hear ever fade from their memory? And how do the people involved—living victims, loved ones, law enforcement—deal with the one who got away?

Most policing districts throughout Canada keep weekly crime statistics for their areas. Some even publish that information. For example, during the week of November 16 to November 22, 2009, RCMP in Red Deer, Alberta, reported a total of 621 calls for service. Some of those calls included 96 bylaw complaints; 52 complaints of mischief; 43 thefts; 31 suspicious person, vehicle or activity calls; 32 calls dealing with assault; 16 drug investigations; 15 domestic violence calls; 11 residential break and enters, while another two involved businesses; six auto thefts; five fraud and one robbery. A lot of what happens during a "normal" week, like the one just described, is dealt with on a case-by-case basis. Even in the more serious matters, when a suspect is not yet in custody, his or her identity and whereabouts are often known.

But at those times when a perpetrator is at large, the police turn to the public for information. They still compose and distribute the familiar wanted posters, though those posters have evolved considerably since the time when they contained triple-decker headlines and paragraphs full of small print and minute details. These days, a large, prominent mug shot of the suspect is usually front and centre, along with a name, a brief description and a contact number for anyone wanting to report seeing the individual. Television and the Internet are also used to publicize information when a criminal is on the loose. Social media networks such as Facebook, for example, have become meeting places for victims of crime and people in various areas of law enforcement. With all that officials have at their disposal, it's becoming increasingly difficult for fugitives to hide, and yet they manage to evade capture for weeks or months. In some cases, years pass, and the suspect in question remains at large, and the alleged crimes go unpunished, leaving victims to struggle with painful memories and an absence of closure.

Like the intricate web of deceit a criminal weaves in the commission of a crime, the stories in this volume are never straightforward. Some convicts can be easily categorized as being purely evil, but others can strike a chord of sympathy. While it's certainly true that we all have the option to choose which path we'll take in life and that breaking the law requires some form of punishment, what some individuals have had to overcome just to remain "normal" is incomprehensible. From childhood sexual abuse to forced prostitution and total neglect, young impressionable minds raised in depraved circumstances can't help but find themselves desperate—and desperation can breed all kinds of maleficent actions.

In the end, writing this book has reinforced one sad truth about life: there is so much pain everywhere, and the pain that some people inflict upon others usually multiplies and infects the lives of the innocent.

At the same time, regardless the trials we face throughout our lives, we still own the ability to choose. No one can take that away from us.

Part One

STILL WANTED

~

Murder. Home invasions. Break and enter. Kidnapping. Rape. Assault. When we hear about these crimes, it disturbs us. When we hear about one of these transgressions being committed in our own neighbourhood, it strikes fear into us. When we learn that the perpetrators of these crimes aren't behind bars but are instead running free and at liberty to possibly strike again, it's terrifying.

Sometimes the work of a serial killer and rapist goes unconnected until the perpetrator is behind bars. Such was the case of Robert William Pickton of Port Coquitlam, British Columbia. A polite and proper Canadian public was aghast at the knowledge that a monster was in their midst. Thankfully, by the time his crimes were made public, he was a suspect in the murders of several of Vancouver's Downtown Eastside prostitutes. But what about those criminals who lurk in the darkness, unidentified, and remain threats to society?

Usually, a serial offender of any kind targets a certain segment of the population. This was certainly true for Richard

Earl Rupert. Seniors, vulnerable and unsuspecting, are his victims of choice. But he's a transient sort and doesn't stick to one city or region. His victims—well, they can sometimes be forgetful. And they're traditionally trusting. Even when the suspect's picture was captured through various surveillance videos and publicized over television newscasts and broadsheets across the country, the kind of people Rupert allegedly targeted didn't expect to be taken by one of Canada's most wanted criminals. Understanding that, someone like Rupert is able to take advantage of these people over and over again. Or could someone we trust, someone who purports to be a friend and confidant, like Fred Siebolt Hofman did, take advantage of our good graces and assault our pocketbooks and bank accounts?

Criminals such as Kevin Vermette and Ronald Bax are a little different. Because their crimes could be categorized as personal vendettas, the general public might not be overwhelmed with fear for their individual safety. Still, Vermette, for example, allegedly displayed an extreme reaction to what he perceived as a personal attack that resulted in three dead and one critically wounded youth. Could someone like that explode without direct provocation and lash out at a total stranger?

Currently, dozens of criminals suspected of all manner of illegal activities haven't been apprehended by the law and, therefore, remain a threat to us all. Thankfully, Canadians aren't usually looking over their shoulders like our neighbours to the south might do from time to time. However, the people on our Most Wanted list represent a real risk to the safety and well-being of our citizens.

Midsummer Massacre
Kevin Vermette

~

He just started firing at us. The first reaction I had was to just run. I started running and just remember getting hit and falling to the ground. I just remember lying there.

–Donny Oliveira, *The Province*, June 11, 1998

When *Edmonton Sun* journalist Keith Bradford interviewed Donny Oliveira in November 2004, what Donny really wanted was closure, a final chapter to a nightmare that began in the summer of 1997 when he was 20 years old. The only way he thought he could get that closure was by finding the man who caused the nightmare, and Oliveira didn't much care if that man was found dead or alive.

For what seemed like an eternity after he'd been shot, Oliveira spent every waking moment reliving whatever details he could recall of a bad dream he could never wake up from. He couldn't get the *pock, pock, pock* sound of a shotgun firing over and over again out of his mind. He recalled seeing the strange man he'd known only in passing and through stories and rumours that meandered their way around town every now and again. Oliveira wasn't sure why the man was there and why he was carrying a shotgun. It seemed incomprehensible that the shots Oliveira heard had come from the man's gun. And yet, he saw the man take aim and chase Oliveira and his three friends through the woods.

The flight response kicked in, and Oliveira bolted. With no clear direction or plan in mind, he just ran, propelled by his own pounding heart, until he fell into the tall grasses carpeting the area around Kitimat. Then everything went dark as the forest floor beneath him turned red with his own blood.

Oliveira heard a different sound when he regained consciousness in a hospital bed. The pulsating beep of monitors replaced the sound of gunfire, and busy nurses were now the ones rushing about. He tried to orient himself to his surroundings. Snatches of the terrifying episode played over and over again in his mind, and like most nightmares, nothing made sense. But waking up in the hospital with a throbbing ache radiating throughout his shattered body and the tubes entering and exiting at various points left no doubt that something terrible had happened. The bad dream wasn't a dream after all, but the full reality of the situation had yet to kick in.

Nobody wanted to tell him what had happened. Oliveira eventually understood the apprehension his family and friends uniformly shared—learning the truth about how he ended up in the hospital and piecing together the nightmare that wouldn't end was even more shattering than his physical injuries. But when

Oliveira's cousin finally stepped up to the plate and delivered the devastating news, Oliveira was overcome with a gut-wrenching combination of anger and agony. Nothing would ever be the same again; the events of that July day in the northern British Columbian wilderness would haunt him for the rest of his life.

That is why Oliveira consented to the interview with Bradford—he craved some kind of closure. Sure, telling his story would never alter the reality of his situation, but it would provide some measure of relief. All Oliveira wanted was for someone to apprehend the man responsible for the hell he shared with so many people.

Long before trappers, adventurers and the missionaries that followed them migrated to the lush forests surrounding the community of Kitimat, the Haisla First Nation called the area home. Although in winter, several dozen centimetres of snow typically layer the ground in any given year, the season is relatively mild in comparison with the barren lands of the far north or the cold and windy prairies of central Canada. Not only was the land picturesque, nestled alongside the Douglas Channel, but it also was habitable even in our country's harshest winters.

And with the area's old-growth forest and its rich natural resources, companies like Alcan and Eurocan set up operations in the mid-1990s and began harvesting the many minerals and forest products available, converting those raw materials into aluminum or pulp and paper. But even before mining and forestry moved in to reap the benefits offered in the region, the Haisla worked the land, gathering food, hunting moose and deer, and fishing for salmon.

This was exactly the kind of place that attracted Kevin Louis Vermette. Most who knew the Jasper-born man considered him polite enough, a hard worker who loved classic cars, and described him as an "avid outdoorsman" and "skilled survivalist" who was well acquainted with the surrounding wilderness. He was quiet, and aside from a dog that was a constant companion until it demonstrated any kind of disobedience and was consequently, immediately replaced, he preferred his own company to that of other people. One Kitimat resident told *The Province* that he'd met Vermette "six or seven years ago and I never saw anybody with him." Vermette's reputation as a recluse was well established throughout the community.

He was also in prime physical condition and maintained a regular workout schedule, often frequenting the local gym. According to information eventually gathered by investigators and reporters, it was during one of those workout sessions that the seeds were planted for what would be described as one of the most heinous massacres the area had ever seen.

For Michael Mauro, 20; David Nunes, 21; Mark Teves, 20; and Donny Oliveira, the summer of 1997 was supposed to be a time for making memories. The four young men were on the brink of manhood and were starting to build lives for themselves. They were full of the energy that only youth can provide—the kind of energy that can sometimes be misunderstood.

Apparently, their exuberance rubbed 42-year-old Vermette the wrong way, especially when it came to the youths' taste in music. The first altercation between the four friends and Vermette allegedly stemmed from Vermette's complaint about the loud rap music they played while working out at the Riverview Recreation Centre in April of that year. (Some reports suggest there were as many as three angry exchanges, with Vermette's temper escalating with each encounter.)

It wasn't the first time Vermette's hot-headedness drew attention. The loner was known for wanting to run things his way, and when his stubbornness came up against opposition, the friction usually led to some kind of encounter. It was just that kind of disposition that led the Kitimat Valley Fitness Centre to allegedly bar him from the club.

However, the exchange between the young men and Vermette didn't appear to raise any unusual concern among the four friends. Mauro's father, Frank, later stated that his son never even mentioned Vermette—he certainly would have if the altercation had disturbed him in any way. For anyone witnessing the exchange at the time, Vermette's extreme behaviour reinforced what many local residents believed—the man was eccentric and quick-tempered, and although he had been accused of uttering threats before, he was generally harmless.

The entire community would have their thoughts about Vermette challenged in ways they could never have imagined.

Saturday, July 12, 1997, was supposed to be a memorable one for Nunes, Mauro, Oliveira and Teves. That night, the four men and their friends were going to let loose a little and help one of their buddies celebrate the last vestiges of his life as a bachelor. Their thoughts were focused on the evening's stag party as they pulled into Hirsch Creek Park to toss a Frisbee around before driving on to Terrace, 70 kilometres north of Kitimat, for the night's festivities.

Unlike the four young men, Vermette was not in a playful mood. According to some reports, he woke up that morning to find the tires on his red Chevy pickup slashed; other accounts suggest that the slashed tires were on his prized 1940s vintage car. Although that kind of discovery would put a damper on anyone's day, Vermette's reaction was extreme. Murdo Macdonald, the owner of the Kitimat Motel where Vermette had lived for the previous seven years and worked as a handyman, told reporters the man he knew was a quiet, loner type of guy. Macdonald said that when Vermette saw his tires, he was enraged, saying he'd kill the person or persons responsible for the vandalism. Macdonald waved off the threats, telling Vermette that he was exaggerating.

He tried to calm Vermette down, but the other man's rage continued to build: "You don't know me, Murdo. I'll kill them."

Although it was never proven, Vermette believed he knew who was responsible for cutting his tires—he was certain it was the work of the four young men from the gym. When Oliveira and his buddies pulled into Hirsch Creek Park, Vermette was following close behind, bent on getting his revenge.

"He parked his truck right in front of our car and got out," Oliveira told Bradford in 2004. "He didn't say a word. He had his shotgun in his hand, and he started shooting."

Vermette was both quick and accurate. Two of the young men weren't able to get out of the car before they were shot dead. Oliveira and another buddy, one report suggests it was Mauro, started running. "The first reaction I had was to just run. I started running and just remember getting hit and falling to the ground," Oliveira told *Province* reporter Lora Grindlay in 1998. "I just remember lying there."

Oliveira knew he'd been shot; he could feel his shirt wet against his chest where he thought he might have been hit. For almost an hour, the young man slipped in and out of consciousness until help finally arrived.

It was too late for Nunes, Teves and Mauro.

Not far away from where the boys had stopped for their game of Frisbee, four fishermen were also looking forward to a memorable weekend. Hoping for a big catch and a whale of a fishing tale to take back home with them, the friends were planning the next day's agenda and getting ready to settle in for the night when they heard the sound of a shotgun firing. It's unclear if these fishermen were the same individuals referred to as the "witnesses" who saw Vermette's truck follow the young men into the park, but they did call the RCMP and report that they'd heard between 8 and 10 shotgun blasts. When police arrived at the park, they discovered four young men whose bodies were riddled with bullet holes.

Nunes, Teves and Mauro were dead. Oliveira was holding onto life by a thread. The lives of countless people were shattered, and the sense of calm that the area's residents felt was destroyed. The RCMP from the otherwise quiet community of Kitimat, with its roughly 12,000 inhabitants, found themselves on what for some would become the biggest case of their career.

While medical personnel tried to stabilize Oliveira so he could be airlifted to a Vancouver hospital, the families of all four men were learning about the tragedy and drowning in an overwhelming tidal wave of grief and disbelief. RCMP emergency responders were dispatched to the Kitimat motel where Vermette lived. Guests at the motel were quickly evacuated and the entire establishment surrounded. Throughout the night, police repeatedly tried to contact Vermette, but it wasn't until eight o'clock the following morning that they stormed his room and discovered he was gone.

The RCMP launched a full-scale search of the area. Anyone familiar with Kitimat knows that aside from travelling by train, there are two main ways into town: the north-south route of Highway 37 that leads to the city of Terrace and by boat along the Douglas Channel. Aside from that, there were just miles and miles of mountainous, wintry wilderness. Even though police didn't think Vermette could get very far on foot, checkstops were established along the highway, and the port area was checked.

While ground crews beat the bushes throughout Kitimat and the surrounding forests, dog teams were brought in to hopefully pick up a scent trail of the wanted man. It seemed only a matter of time before Vermette, who'd apparently fled on foot with little more than the clothes on his back, his shotgun and his dog, was apprehended.

But Vermette was about to surprise the community once again.

In the days and weeks following the killings, a small army of roughly 20 law enforcement personnel worked around the clock looking for the suspected murderer. Helicopters equipped with infrared heat-sensing devices scoured the thick forests throughout the Regional District of Kitimat-Stikine, venturing as far away as Terrace in the hope of uncovering something that might suggest Vermette's location. It seemed inconceivable that the man could disappear without a trace, and Kitimat's RCMP Sergeant Jim Howie went on record as saying there was "no reason to believe [Vermette had] left the area." And yet, none of the RCMP's efforts uncovered any trace of the wanted man.

As posters were put up across BC and into neighbouring provinces, the concern Kitimat residents felt that an alleged murderer was still at large reverberated throughout the Northwest. Vermette was described as being 5-feet-10 and weighing about 150 pounds. He wore glasses and had several distinctive tattoos: a cat captioned "Lucky" on his right arm and a coyote howling at the moon on his left, along with a dagger stuck through a red rose. Residents gathered around community bulletin boards in shopping malls and grocery stores, gazing at images of the man and sharing a mutual disbelief that such a thing could happen in their midst. And when the news broke that the four youths Vermette accused of slashing his tires were cleared of any responsibility in the vandalism, grief over the shootings intensified.

Even more unbelievable was that Vermette remained at large. Northern British Columbia is sparsely populated, and people generally know each other. Strangers in town are noticed, especially those with prominent identifying marks like the tattoos Vermette sported. Photographs of the alleged murderer had been clearly displayed on the wanted posters blanketing the province, and every newspaper and television broadcast showed pictures of the man as well. The U.S. television show *America's Most Wanted* even aired a story on Vermette. And although more than 300 tips flowed into RCMP detachments from as far away as Edmonton, Alberta, not one led to the wanted man.

Despite almost heroic efforts to find Vermette, newspapers following the story reported in their July 26 issues that the search had been scaled back. Even now, investigators don't believe Vermette had fled the area. Instead, it appeared more likely that he was a better survivalist than most gave him credit for. Either that or he may have taken his own life when the full reality of the heinous act he committed hit home. Still, it seemed logical to think that such a thorough investigation would have yielded something, even if it were just a few scattered remains.

For the people of Kitimat, especially the friends and family members of the four young victims in the shootings, some kind of closure was desperately needed.

It took the better part of a year for Oliveira to recover from the physical injuries he received that summer day in 1997. He had to have his spleen surgically removed, along with a portion of his liver. His esophagus, diaphragm, stomach and left arm were all damaged to varying degrees when he was shot in the back, and he underwent several surgeries to repair the injuries.

"I'll never be 100 percent because I have nerve damage in my left arm, and there's a lot of scarring," Oliveira told reporters in 2004. "But I'm doing fairly well."

Kevin Vermette is still listed as one of Canada's most wanted fugitives, and the case remains open and under investigation to this day, albeit on a much smaller scale. Occasionally, larger searches are held. In the fall of 2005, police again scoured the area surrounding Kitimat, but yet again, the search came up empty.

At the time of this writing, more than 13 years after the brutal massacre, not a hint of Vermette, his dog or his weapon has ever been found. He has truly disappeared without a trace. But the memory of what he did will never totally fade away for Oliveira, or for the friends and families of Michael Mauro, David Nunes and Mark Teves. Like many others, they all still cling to the hope that the man who changed their lives forever will one day be found—dead or alive.

The Nephew Bandit
Richard Earl Rupert

~

He's very good at his trade. All the complainants describe him as polite, well spoken. He engages the conversations and makes the complainants feel comfortable with him.... He would actually take them to the bank.

–Detective John Dunlop of the Toronto police major crimes unit to reporters in January 2010

The young man looked nice enough. The tinge of grey to his short, dirty-blond hair and the slightly receding hairline betrayed his age, but his close shave gave his face a youthful look. No one would guess the good-looking gent was in his 50s.

Poor soul. Looks can be so deceiving. At about 5 feet, 6 inches, and weighing between 140 and 160 pounds, he looked healthy and quite capable of holding down a job. However, he seemed to have had a streak of bad luck lately. Perhaps he wasn't as well as he looked?

But he caught a lucky break, by bumping into his elderly great-aunt. The two hadn't seen each other in decades, and yet, he said she remembered his name.

Too bad he couldn't stay longer. His auntie would have loved that.

∽

Unscrupulous culprits have been profiting from an endless variety of cons for as long as human civilization has been in existence. Some of them have even justified their actions by pointing out the victim's responsibility in being conned or deriving some kind of other benefit from their deceit, such as entertainment value, for example.

Phineas Taylor Barnum stated that there was "a sucker born every minute" and that he could take advantage of that vulnerability, combined with visual illusions, to turn a profit. Although one can't place him in the same category as a cold-hearted scam artist prying precious dollars out of a senior's hands, Barnum walked a fine line between honesty and chicanery to make his living.

On the other hand, William "Canada Bill" Jones, arguably one of the greatest three-card-Monte sharks operating in the 1800s, worked his way from his home in Yorkshire, England, to Canada and across the United States, blatantly taking advantage of anyone gullible enough to believe the lies Canada Bill dished out at any given moment. As far as he was concerned, if someone fell for one of his scams, they deserved to suffer from a considerably thinner pocketbook. After all, it was Canada Bill who once said, "It is immoral to let a sucker keep his money."

Throughout human history, people have lost their life savings thinking they'd taken advantage of a great investment opportunity. Others gave in to basic greed, jumping on one of those "too good to be true" opportunities. But there are those who've fallen for the wiles of a smooth talker simply because they're frightened, fragile or too naïve to recognize the wolf beneath the sheep's clothing. These were the type of people that Richard Earl Rupert is accused of targeting over the years, and he has developed a fairly lengthy track record as a scam artist who attacks a particular demographic of the population: the elderly and disabled.

Concerns that Rupert was allegedly on the prowl, looking for trusting and kind-hearted seniors to take advantage of, surfaced after a widely publicized incident that took place in Toronto on November 30, 2009. His name and past history garnered national attention after he was identified as the thug who roughed up an 81-year-old woman while trying to take her purse. The media immediately jumped on the story; they published pictures of video footage from the apartment building foyer that captured the man grabbing the woman's purse and shoving her into a nearby chair.

That's what the video showed, but the information the woman shared involved a more intricate spider web of lies that appalled residents even more. According to the woman's story, the unknown man had approached her earlier that day, saying he was the building manager. He went on to suggest that if she paid her next month's rent in advance, he could provide her with a discount.

The offer sounded reasonable enough—discounts are given for all kinds of reasons. And what senior on a fixed income isn't interested in saving a bit of money? The woman agreed to the arrangement but didn't have the cash on hand. The man accompanied the elderly woman to the bank where she withdrew the money. When they returned to her apartment building, the phony manager asked her for her key. It was a red-flag moment for the senior. What kind of manager doesn't carry a key to the building he is responsible for?

Now suspicious of the man, the woman changed her mind about handing over the cash. The robber then grabbed her purse. The woman might have been an octogenarian, but she stood her ground. She resisted her attacker as the two played tug-of-war over her purse and the money it contained. The man finally pushed the woman into a nearby chair, leaving her and her purse behind as he exited the building. The entire incident in the building's foyer took just over a minute. The officer in charge of the case uploaded the offensive footage onto YouTube in the hope that someone might be able to identify the man.

At first, the woman was reluctant to call the police. She later told reporters that she'd felt foolish for falling for the scam.

But it was because she put aside her pride and reported the incident that it gained a considerable amount of media attention and an outraged public devoured the story. What kind of person takes advantage of an elderly woman? In most people's minds, it wasn't just a robbery that had been committed; it was an offence against humankind on a much broader scale. This opportunist, this pariah, had taken advantage of one of the most vulnerable members of society. Someone like that had to be stopped.

Portions of that same video footage were broadcast on evening newscasts across Toronto, and readers were inhaling the stories running in the city's dailies. The incident sparked all kinds of coffee room and water cooler chatter. But nobody suspected what would come next. Citizens of Toronto were only beginning to learn about a man who had been in their midst and robbing the elderly and disabled for some time. And thanks to the bravery of one vulnerable senior who came forward to share her story, news about this opportunist was about to gain national attention. Unknowingly, the woman had exposed something much larger than a local robbery. She had provided investigators with a link between several similar incidents across Ontario. It was starting to look like the same man who had approached her was responsible for several other similar scams conducted against seniors.

What unfolded continued to shock an unbelieving and disheartened public.

Not long after media reports had filtered throughout Toronto, tips began flowing into the local police. Although increasing public attention and gathering reports from individuals is the ultimate goal of any media plea, the sheer volume of concern the November 30 story amassed likely startled even seasoned officers. And the information they uncovered pointed them in an interesting direction.

It appeared as though the unknown assailant was someone the authorities were familiar with, if only by his method. By connecting the dots between detachments in St. Catharines, Waterloo, London, Ottawa and Thunder Bay, investigators were quite certain the person they were looking for was none other than Richard Earl Rupert.

As the investigation developed, police started plotting Rupert's alleged attacks on a map, dating each one as they went along. Two scams apparently took place in Thunder Bay in January 2008, both involving 83-year-old women. The next incident took place in February 2009, when Rupert hit up an 88-year-old man in Waterloo. On March 15 of that year, he allegedly scammed a 93-year-old man in St. Catharines, and two days later, he was believed to have targeted another 93-year-old male in London.

The first recorded scams in Toronto involved a 93-year-old woman and an 89-year-old man, and both incidents occurred on September 7. From there, it looked as if Rupert moved on to Ottawa and robbed a 92-year-old woman on October 27.

He returned to Toronto in November and allegedly targeted several victims ranging in age from 81 to 94 on November 22, 23, 24 and 30.

The above incidents were the ones police knew of and for which they had video surveillance that showed the suspect they believed to be Rupert. But a man as audacious as that, someone who appeared to make a living by ripping off seniors, could conceivably have attacked countless other victims—victims who, like the November 30 victim, were too embarrassed to come forward.

As police gathered more information on their person of interest and worked with media to provide the public with regular updates, other, more reluctant victims ventured forward to share their stories. Some of Rupert's suspected recent victims were also anxious to talk with the police. And yet, despite the public's interest in the case and the media's willingness to keep their readers and listeners constantly updated with new information, seniors were still being conned. That Rupert continued to run his scams regardless of all the public attention directed his way was brazen to say the least. And to top it all off, he was getting away with his crimes.

As investigators reviewed the case and interviewed victims, it appeared that several factors likely contributed to Rupert's success, beginning with the man himself. With the exception of Rupert's tussle with the 81-year-old woman in the lobby of her residence, he didn't demonstrate a violent nature. He also appeared to be well groomed, and his clothes were in good repair. When he spoke, he was always cordial, gentle and well mannered.

Rupert also presented his victims with an assortment of plausible stories. Sometimes he said he was a distant nephew. Now, by the time someone hits the golden age of 80-something, it's quite possible that the person could conceivably lose track of one or two nephews. And if the story triggered some foggy memory, it's easy to see how anyone might feel some kind of obligation to long-lost kinfolk. At that point, the con man would make himself at home, enjoy a cup of coffee and even look at photo albums with his current victim, making small talk while trying to decide on the most lucrative means of attack or scanning the surroundings for something of value to pilfer.

When presenting himself to a new target, the suspect often did not mention his name, looking, instead, for his victim to suggest one. He might say, "Hi, Uncle, remember me?" The suspect might then ask his targeted victim if he or she remembered that summer vacation a couple of decades back when the suspect and his mother or father stopped by for a visit, or some other typical family situation. The victim might reply, "Ah, you must be Peter," and so the suspect becomes Peter for the day, or at least until he convinces the "aunt" or "uncle" to "loan" him some money for one kind of emergency or another.

One of the favourite emergencies that Rupert allegedly uses to con his victims into handing over large sums of money is for car repairs. It is a variation on the broken-down-car scenario that Rupert reportedly used on one of his 93-year-old male victims in March 2009. In that case, the elderly gentleman was approached in his retirement home. The suspect walked into the residence and confidently honed in on the man. No reasonable-minded person would imagine that a con man would choose that kind of public setting, but that's exactly what he did. After the suspect convinced the old man that he was a distant nephew and fed him the story about the broken-down car, the senior agreed to help him. Not only did the gentleman hand over the cash he had on hand, but he also agreed to go to the bank with his "nephew." The senior withdrew a considerable amount of money, and the con man disappeared soon after driving the gent back to his retirement home.

It was two days before the man's family learned of the deception; perhaps the knowledge that he'd been robbed didn't even occur to the gentleman until his family heard the story and explained that it was a sham. There was no distant nephew, and if there had been, he would have surely contacted other family members instead of an elderly uncle in a retirement home.

Although the man's family contacted the police immediately, enough time had elapsed for them to lose the trail of the suspect. Along with the embarrassment that many of Rupert's alleged victims felt over falling for his ridiculous tales, not recognizing they'd been robbed also delayed the investigation. Still, the law of averages being what it is, if the man purportedly responsible for these robberies continued to ply his trade, it was only a matter of time before the authorities apprehended the criminal.

With each scenario, Rupert was garnering more and more police attention. He was rapidly scaling the ladder of popularity when it came to making a name for himself as one of Canada's most wanted scumbags.

By January 2010, newspapers across the country were running stories on the man who was now being dubbed the "Nephew Bandit." Police in western Canada theorized that Rupert might be headed their way, and officers were anxious to work with the media to alert the public that a con artist zeroing in on vulnerable seniors might be operating nearby. Police asked bank employees to pay particular attention to any seniors coming into their branches accompanied by a younger male with the goal of withdrawing money. Banks were also provided with detailed descriptions of the suspect, along with posters highlighting pictures of the man from several different angles.

While it soon became clear that Rupert was indeed making his way west, at this point in the tale, it looked like the suspect was still in Ontario. On April 10, 2010, Marie White, an Ottawa-area woman, almost handed the Nephew Bandit directly over to the police on a silver platter, so to speak. The woman was enjoying a Saturday evening out with friends at Ottawa's James Street Pub. Flipping through a copy of that day's issue of the *Ottawa Sun,* she noticed a story about the senior scammer. After she finished reading, she glanced up and gasped. "I turned my head and looked towards the screen to watch the game, and the guy is sitting right there, in view of me at the bar," White told reporters.

White was so convinced that the man at the bar was Richard Earl Rupert that she pointed him out to her friends. They agreed with her identification, although some were a little leery about calling the police. But White's mind was made up as soon as her friends agreed that the man sitting an arm's length away definitely resembled the Nephew Bandit. Determined to move on the information, White left the bar and dialled the Crime Stoppers' telephone number provided at the bottom of the article she'd just read. According to White, the woman taking her call seemed confused as to why an Ottawa call was coming through on a Toronto-area line. The operator also appeared reluctant to take any action on the information White was providing and instructed White to call the police. Then the line went dead. White believed the woman hung up on her; the authorities later said the call was somehow disconnected. Either way, a frustrated White returned to the pub without being able to connect with the police.

A few hours later, White walked out of the bar not far behind the suspect. She yelled out the suspect's name. "Rupert!" she said. White told reporters that she believed the man tried to see who was calling him. Later that evening, White eventually talked with the police, but by then the suspect was long gone. The smooth-talking senior scammer had slipped away, once again.

By now, Rupert's routine was pretty clear to the authorities. The man, who appeared to bed down at a variety of hostels, hotels or bed and breakfasts, didn't stay in any one place for long. It looked like he would orchestrate a robbery or two in any given area until he felt the police had been alerted to his presence, and then he'd move on to a new location. The authorities believed Rupert was originally from Windsor, and although he'd lived in several Ontario communities, he wasn't a stranger to western Canada.

In April 2008, a 90-year-old in West Vancouver had been the target of one of Rupert's alleged schemes. Rupert's apparent migration to the west could explain the time gap between the two senior scams he'd been connected to in Thunder Bay in January 2008 and the other frauds he'd allegedly committed in Ontario in January 2009.

However, a closer look at Rupert's past unveiled further connections with the west. A Saskatchewan *Star Phoenix* news report dated July 3, 1997, gave a detailed account of Rupert's activities more than a decade earlier—activities that landed the 54-year-old in jail. The story highlighted how Rupert "pleaded guilty to 13 counts of fraud and theft under $500." In these cases, he admitted to stealing more than $3000 between May 1996 and March 1997. The crimes were committed in Regina and Saskatoon, and Rupert's victims were nine seniors, ranging from 70 to 100 years of age. In many of the 13 crimes to which Rupert had pleaded guilty, he either posed as a distant relative in need of money to fix a car or start a business. In at least one of these cases, he emptied a woman's purse when she left the room to call a relative and check out Rupert's story. "He has preyed on the weaknesses of our senior citizens. They don't deserve to lose all their life savings through this type of trickery," charged Eric Neufeld, the Crown prosecutor in the 1997 proceedings.

Rupert's guilty plea earned him three years in jail, but that decision likely saved him more than it cost since several other charges were stayed as a result of his cooperation. Neufeld had asked for a sentence of between four and five years, but Maria Pappas, Rupert's defence attorney at the time, effectively argued her client's case. She told the court that her client's cooperation should be rewarded. She also reminded the court that Rupert had special considerations himself—he was a diagnosed schizophrenic and hadn't been violent when committing his crimes. Clearly, Pappas' plea made an impression on Judge Diane Morris, but she didn't let Rupert go without a verbal reprimand, "These acts you committed are shameful. It's absolutely reprehensible to prey on people who may be living on fixed incomes."

That same *Star Phoenix* news report also made reference to Rupert's "previous record of 53 convictions." At least some of those convictions stemmed from a scam operating in Vancouver a decade earlier, from August 1986 to January 1987. At that time, Rupert was arrested following an investigation into several complaints of fraud, and he eventually pleaded guilty to six Criminal Code fraud offences and was sentenced to three months in jail. It appears that Rupert's habit of introducing himself to various seniors as their "nephew" was firmly established even then. He reportedly contacted his victims, usually women, via telephone, and after a brief chat during which he'd explain how he'd been ill and needed some financial help, he would convince these people to loan him money. After getting the cash, the senior and Rupert would typically part ways, with Rupert promising that his mother would "pay them back."

At the time of that conviction, other complaints had been lodged against Rupert. However, these individuals didn't press charges because some of them were too ill, others struggled with memory problems and still others were just downright frightened. And while Rupert's reputation as a "gentleman" who pulled off these cons without resorting to violence was somewhat intact, Sergeant Larry Richardson told the *Vancouver Sun* in November 1987 that "one victim was so traumatized that she moved back to the Prairies and died shortly afterward."

Rupert may not have caused any bodily harm, but clearly the emotional impact of his actions had an effect on his victims' overall health and well-being.

In 1987, Rupert was also wanted on similar charges in Winnipeg. And although he'd already faced off with the law in that city, it didn't seem to preclude his return.

Headlines suggesting that Toronto's Nephew Bandit had been spotted in Winnipeg or was tied to "rip-offs of one or more in Manitoba" blazed across the city's dailies on June 11 and 12, 2010. A bank manager at the HSBC branch at 330 St. Mary's Avenue was the first to contact police, saying she was certain the man pictured on a wanted poster in the bank's lunchroom had visited her branch on Friday, June 4. An elderly man was trying to withdraw some money from the branch's ATM at around five o'clock that evening. A younger man was hovering over his shoulder, and it looked as if he was instructing the senior on what to do. When the manager moved closer, she immediately recognized the younger man as Richard Earl Rupert, whose image had graced the staff's lunchroom since January.

The next day, another story in the *Winnipeg Sun* focused on an incident that occurred on Wednesday, June 10. Rupert allegedly "befriended" a 75-year-old man while visiting him at his home. Constable Natalie Aitken told reporters that Rupert gained entry into the senior's suite by saying he was a relative.

At some point during the visit, the suspect reportedly stole a small amount of money before fleeing. Luckily, an on-site video surveillance camera captured the image of the man scanning the tenant directory. That man was none other than Richard Earl Rupert.

By now, investigators had connected Rupert to at least two other senior scams reported in Winnipeg in 2009. With all levels of law enforcement across the country on alert for the man, it was hard to imagine how Rupert continued to evade capture—and yet so far he had.

If Detective John Dunlop of the Toronto Police Service has any say in the matter, Rupert's luck will run out sooner than later. "He's been lucky so far, but his time is running out," Dunlop told reporters from the FOX television series, *America's Most Wanted*. Rupert acquired the unique distinction of being one of the few Canadians to make it on the show in 2010—the episode featuring Rupert ran on September 25. "He's hard to track because he doesn't have a driver's licence, he travels everywhere by bus, and he always pays in cash," Dunlop said.

Rupert also has a reputation for repeating his long-lost relative routine—a routine that's served him well over the years. "You read the reports from the different jurisdictions, and it's almost as if the same author wrote everything," Dunlop said. Reports about Rupert's exploits suggest that his first crime was committed when he was a 14-year-old paperboy and noticed how easy it was to rip off some of his elderly customers.

The Nephew Bandit
RICHARD EARL RUPERT

The Nephew Bandit has proven to be skilled in assessing the most vulnerable members of society. By targeting seniors, he is tapping into a segment of the population that operates under a somewhat different set of standards than many younger individuals. The elderly are more trusting and more willing to help someone in need, whereas Rupert's peers and those younger are typically more suspicious. Even one-time professionals, like the 96-year-old former college professor who was allegedly approached by Rupert in his Toronto retirement home, have been taken in by the man's gentle, easy manner and charisma. The senior had believed the suspect's story that he was a nephew because the elderly man was expecting a visit from a distant relative at the time. "I gave him $200 with the understanding, I suppose, that he'd pay it back sometime," said the senior. But it was more than just believing in the lines Rupert delivered. "Part of it was, in the old army days, if another enlisted man says, 'Look, I need some help,' you help him out if you can."

The *America's Most Wanted* episode airing the Nephew Bandit garnered even more interest from Canadian officials. On hearing the story, Burnaby RCMP suspected that Rupert might have been involved in a reported theft on September 7, 2010. Media reports about the con man and his exploits continue to inform a large portion of the Canadian public who might not be aware of him. With Rupert's nomadic tendencies, it's important that news about the man remain on the national stage. And as the heat turns up on the investigation,

American officials are also on the lookout for the suspect should he decide to try his hand at a similar scam south of the border.

At the time of this writing, Rupert is wanted by police for a long list of crimes, including robbery, break and enter, and fraud. With any luck, by the time this book hits store shelves, unsuspecting seniors won't have to worry about being taken advantage of by Richard Earl Rupert.

A Shot in the Dark
Ronald Jeffrey Bax

The small community of Carcross, Yukon Territory, is known for its summer solstice midnight sun hike, its UFO sightings, the Tagish Lake meteor that exploded over the community on January 18, 2000, and the infamous Polly the Parrot that watched over the guests at the Caribou Hotel for 126 years before the old bird passed away in 1972.

Located a stone's throw from British Columbia's northern border, the village had been the traditional home of the Tlingit and Tagish people who hunted and fished in the region long before the first modern village was established in 1896. It was originally named Caribou Crossing, after the numerous caribou that migrated through the area, but the name was condensed to its current form in 1904, primarily to ease mail delivery—Caribou was a common name in neighbouring Alaska, British Columbia and throughout the Yukon, and the post office thought the name change would reduce the chance for confusing address locations.

Carcross is located along the major South Klondike Highway, between Bennett and Nares lakes, about 75 kilometres southeast of Whitehorse. During the Klondike Gold Rush, prospectors anxious to hit the motherlode drifted through the community in large numbers, drawn by the promise of striking it rich. When the rush was over, the crowds of people living in the area thinned considerably, but enough stayed to make the community viable.

By 1992, about 300 residents called Carcross home. Some came to visit—tourism is a mainstay of the village's economy, especially during prime summer months—while others chose to live there permanently because of the surrounding wilderness and natural beauty. It was a place of solitude, a place where people could really think and find themselves. It was also a close-knit community where everyone knew and looked out for one another the way a large family would.

Krystal Senyk, an Ontario girl from St. Catharines, made her initial stop in Carcross to visit her dear friend, Lynn Blaikie Bax. The two women knew each other from St. Catharines—Lynn had lived there before moving to Carcross with her husband, Ronald, and the couple's two children.

What brought the Baxes to a corner of the world so far removed from their extended family isn't clear. But gauging by Ronald's interest in the fields of guide outfitting and taxidermy, one presumes the outdoors was the primary drawing card. The same was true for Krystal. It didn't take her long to fall in love with the place when she visited in 1988. The beauty and solitude captivated her. And so she stayed and made a home for herself in Carcross. Lynn was likely thrilled to have her friend join her in the northern wilderness, where the small population limits the number of friendships one can make.

Krystal Senyk was young, smart and talented. By 1992, she was holding down a position as a federal government land claims negotiator. She was also very active, had fun taking part in community activities and, in 1990, earned the title of Canadian women's arm wrestling champion. All in all, she enjoyed her new life and her new home in Carcross.

But when Krystal moved north in 1988, she couldn't have foreseen how that decision would so permanently and unforgivingly wipe out any hopes and dreams she might have had for her future.

Carcross is still a frozen wasteland in March. Although the sun tries to spread its warmth, it's not strong enough to melt away the winter snow. It was certainly chilly that evening in 1992 as Krystal Senyk walked up her sidewalk to the front door of her cabin on Taggish Road. She pulled her coat closer and was perhaps a little distracted by her visit with Lynn as she fumbled for the keys in her pocket with cold fingers. She probably didn't see him, didn't even know he was there until she heard a sharp sound shatter the night silence.

Police later said that Krystal was gunned down around 11:00 PM on March 1, 1992. Someone had been lying in wait for her, someone patient enough to sit tight and hardy enough to withstand the evening chill. He was also some kind of a marksman—one shot to the back of the head with a high-calibre weapon was all it took to kill the 29-year-old. The gunshot wound indicated that the shooter was relatively close to his victim when he fired; he must have emerged suddenly from the cover of darkness, moving quickly to take aim on the unarmed woman. The kill shot was swift and accurate—the sign of a hunter well schooled in his craft.

Senyk died a brave woman. While news of her murder initially rocked the tightly knit community, the shock quickly faded away as information about the woman and her actions just before the shooting emerged. It appeared she wasn't only courageous but was also a hero in her own right.

Suspicion for the murder immediately fell on Senyk's neighbour, Ronald Jeffrey Bax. It's always difficult when tensions rise between neighbours, and the situation between Senyk and Bax was particularly dangerous. There was talk that Bax and his wife, Lynn, had been struggling with marital problems for some time—problems that Bax allegedly believed Senyk exacerbated.

As far as Senyk was concerned, her influence on Lynn's life was far from overwhelming. In fact, Senyk probably wished Lynn would pay more attention to the anxiety she felt regarding her friend's marriage. Still, Senyk had recently had dangerous, ugly threats made against her, and she was becoming more than a little worried.

Word had it that Bax believed Senyk was a lesbian and that she was encouraging his wife to leave him. Some of the tongue wagging in town just after Senyk's murder suggested that Bax had been trying to drown his sorrows at the Caribou Hotel and was uttering more and more threats against Senyk with each glass he downed. The story, "Notes on Loving Your Neighbour," written by Harris Taylor, recounted some of the alleged conversation that night at the bar just prior to the attack on Senyk. "I'm going to clean up this territory, kill those man-hating lesbians. Cops won't ever find me," Bax allegedly threatened.

But Bax's anger was misplaced, or at the very least misinformed. Senyk was supporting her friend's decision to leave Bax but not because she was a "man-hating lesbian." Senyk was just a strong woman who knew her value and wouldn't put up with the kind of abuse her friend Lynn was apparently living through. It was Bax's temperament, his nasty threats and the mean way he treated Lynn and the children that prompted Senyk to back her friend's decision to finally pack her bags and leave the man.

Senyk had spent the weekend helping Lynn Bax and her children settle into a nearby safe haven for women escaping from a violent home life. Senyk had been Lynn's only visitor that

Sunday night. Her warm offer of friendship must have brought a great deal of comfort to Lynn's stressful situation. The next morning, whatever comfort Senyk had provided quickly evaporated, and Lynn's life circumstances would become even more troubling.

Shortly after police discovered Krystal Senyk's crumpled body, attention turned to Ronald Bax. Rumour and innuendo might not hold up in a court of law, but they are sometimes the stepping stones needed to lead investigators to the truth. But when officers knocked on Ronald's front door and he didn't answer, they were left with an uneasy feeling. A quick search of the premises led police to think that some of Ronald's guns might be missing, and the dirty-blond, somewhat rugged-looking, 30-year-old outdoorsman known for his survival skills and marksmanship was nowhere to be found.

Because the authorities suspected that Bax was responsible for Senyk's death, and reflecting on his skill with weapons, his alleged state of mind and the tensions in his relationship with his wife, police sequestered 16 people whom they felt might be in some danger from him. Among those individuals under police protection were Lynn and her two children. Whitehorse RCMP Sergeant Bill Cameron told reporters that the individuals in protection were "people that had direct contact with the Bax family and were directly or indirectly involved with the marriage breakup."

A Shot in the Dark
RONALD JEFFREY BAX

By now, several days had passed with still no sign of Ronald Bax. The neighbouring communities of Skagway and Haines were alerted about the murder, and officials there were also on the lookout for Bax. A Canada-wide warrant for Bax's arrest was issued, and his face was plastered on posters across the country. And although there are a lot of blond-haired, blue-eyed men who are 5-feet, 7-inches tall and weigh about 150 pounds, Bax had one unique identifying feature he couldn't easily hide—the tattoo of a winged horse on his upper right arm. Bax was now a wanted man, and the charge against him was one of first-degree murder. Police believed he was quite possibly armed and dangerous, and they were warning people to avoid any contact with the man should they think they'd spotted him in their neighbourhood.

The police never located Bax. It was as if he had disappeared. Was it true what Bax said that night at the Caribou Hotel—that the cops would never find him?

In September 1992, the *Hamilton Spectator* reported that the Yukon's chief coroner, Jean Veinott, was meeting with other officials to decide if they should convene an inquest into Senyk's death. Six months had passed since the March shooting, and the investigation into the murder was no longer active. The authorities had tracked every possibility they could think of and still hadn't turned up any solid leads in the case. They'd checked out Ronald's connections in Ontario, in the interior of BC, and explored the possibility that he might have crossed the border and joined relatives in Michigan. The syndicated shows *Unsolved Mysteries* and *America's Most Wanted* at one point aired segments on the story. The FBI cooperated with the Canadian authorities in advertising the man's most wanted status. Even Bax's immediate family near Walkerton, Ontario, went public, pleading that Ronald turn himself in to the authorities.

While the RCMP continued to look for Bax and publicize the case, an already overloaded system was being further overwhelmed with other crimes, and resources were stretched thin. The case had gone cold, and much to the heartbreak of those involved, it seemed quite possible that someone could get away with murder.

An inquest isn't the same as a trial, but it would provide an opportunity for officials to look for flaws in the legal system. "The job of the coroner is to find out what happened, to bring details forward as the victims are not able to speak for themselves," Veinott told reporters. "We need answers as the details in this death are rather nebulous. We don't have sufficient information to establish definite circumstances prior to the death."

Were Lynn and her children adequately supported and counselled during the marriage breakup? Did anyone take the threats made to Krystal Senyk seriously? Had Ronald Bax ever been confronted about his alleged abuse? Did he receive any kind of counselling to deal with his feelings of anger and rejection? And what, if anything, could have been done to prevent the tragedy?

Whatever happened to Ronald Bax is still unknown. Is he living the life of a mountain man, squatting in the wilderness and surviving off the land? Or did he make a clean getaway and start new somewhere else? Is he still alive? If he is alive, do any of those 16 people who were once placed under police protection still need to be concerned for their safety? Did Bax die while he was on the run? Could he have committed suicide?

The final chapter of this case has yet to be written, and in the eyes of the law, Ronald Bax deserves his day in court and is innocent until proven guilty. On the other hand, those associated with the crime believe they know who Senyk's killer is. As for Bax, he has managed to have the last word—the police still haven't found him.

"Man of God" Too Good to Be True
Fred Siebolt Hofman

~

> *He's been described as "one of the great escape artists" of Canadian crime, a former Vancouver investment adviser alleged to have fleeced dozens of BC residents of their life savings before slipping out of sight nearly 20 years ago—just ahead of an RCMP arrest warrant on 61 counts of fraud and theft totalling $10 million...*
>
> *–The Vancouver Sun*, April 28, 2007

The Christian Reformed Church in Canada traces its roots back to the Dutch Reformed Church in the Netherlands. Having officially established itself in Emden, Germany, in October 1571, the Dutch Reformed Church followed heavily the tutelage of John Calvin, a leading theologian of the Protestant Reformation whose teachings focused on God's sovereign grace and the principles of salvation through Jesus Christ.

As with most Christian denominations and religious philosophies, the Dutch Reformed Church has evolved over the intervening years between its inception and the present day. As Dutch settlers moved to North America in the 17th century, they brought with them the tenets of a faith whose fabric was so tightly woven with ethnic tradition that it inevitably spoke almost as deeply of a way of life as it did about belief principles. For example, sending children to government-run schools wasn't something many Dutch immigrants were comfortable with, and so Christian schools grew up alongside the churches that supported them, and the Christian Reformed Church became a leader in Christian-based education.

But life in a new world came with growing pains. In 1857, another reformation of sorts took place, this time within the newly established traditions developed in the freshly formed denomination, and Grand Rapids, Michigan, was the first site for the original church of the Christian Reformed Church, an independent branch of the Dutch Reformed Church. With a new name and renewed vigour, it wasn't long before the forward-looking faith community was founding additional parishes across the United States and in Canada. In 1905, Alberta became home to one of the first Christian Reformed churches in this country; the denomination grew rapidly, with a second parish opening its doors in Winnipeg just six years later. More congregations soon followed, and on October 21, 1926, the First Christian Reformed Church opened its doors in Vancouver, British Columbia, making history as the first church of that denomination in Canada's westernmost province.

For almost a century now, new Dutch immigrants moving into BC have turned to the First Christian Reformed

Church and its sister parishes across the province. In a time of change, where a new way of life replaced the familiar customs of home, newcomers almost uniformly turned to their beloved church for a sense of stability and a place from which to gain comfort by sharing a common belief system and customs.

At one time, Dutch Canadian Fred Siebolt Hofman was one of those newcomers. Hofman was born on April 12, 1937, in the community of Veenwouden, in the province of Friesland, Netherlands, and then moved to British Columbia with his family in the early 1950s. The teen became a man in his newfound home, finished his schooling in Canada and acquired his post-secondary education. In the early 1970s, Hofman became a Certified General Accountant (CGA) and established an accounting practice. Along with the routine work of any CGA, some of the Hofman's responsibilities included his role as an investment counsellor, and he often traded securities on the Vancouver Stock Exchange (VSE). All in all, his accomplishments in his new homeland would have pleased most young men his age.

Hofman was also comfortably rooted in the church of his heritage, a membership he was clearly proud of (as of this writing, he has never relinquished his Dutch citizenship). As a long-time member of Vancouver's First Christian Reformed Church, the same church that cemented the denomination's presence in British Columbia, Hofman considered himself a faithful steward, a "man of God," as it were. As was common among what some

"Man of God" Too Good to Be True
FRED SIEBOLT HOFMAN

church analysts refer to as "A-list members"—those who've remained committed to their faith community over many years and even generations—it was only natural that the CGA would continue on in yet another long-standing tradition of his ancestors and not only worship in the faith practices of his homeland, but also serve his church in some manner.

It made sense then, that the man with a knack for numbers and a heart for his church community would offer his services to fill the role of church treasurer when the position fell vacant. One source described the blue-eyed, blond-haired gentleman with the receding hairline, who stood an imposing 6 feet, one inch and weighed in at a healthy 231 pounds, as "affable." He was the kind of man who knew how to put people at ease, which was a particularly strong trait when it came to his role as an investment counsellor. After all, most of us are a little leery when it comes to risking our hard-earned income, but by most accounts, Hofman had a way of alleviating the worry and reassuring his clients.

With more than 20 years of living and worshipping with the people of First Christian Reformed Church, and after spending a great many of those years serving as the parish's moneyman, it made sense that the gent with a keen eye for an opportunity chose to build at least part of his client base there. Most of his fellow parishioners believed that if they couldn't trust a man like Hofman, they couldn't trust anybody. Even those who were reluctant to place their savings into what might arguably have appeared to be risky investments believed that Hofman knew what he was doing when he suggested one stock option or another. With few exceptions, anyone in the position to take Hofman up on one of his suggestions placed their cash, along with their trust, in the outwardly jolly fellow.

They were about to discover that a more sinister Mr. Hyde was lurking beneath the garb of what everyone thought was a kinder, softer Dr. Jekyll.

Authorities began a serious review of Hofman's accounting business between 1985 and 1991. But that wasn't the first time watchdogs who monitored the practices of British Columbia's CGAs were alerted to the suggestion that something was a little off about the man. He had by then had charmed a long list of clients. In fact, concerns about Hofman's ethics dated as far back as the mid-1960s, when Hofman had founded what he called an "investment club." One Dutch Canadian professional referred to in the media simply as "Binne" explained how he and four other men helped Hofman lay the groundwork for this rudimentary group in 1965.

According to one news story, Binne and his colleagues each invested $500 with the man who had an eye for opportunity. Apparently Hofman had drawn up a 10-point document outlining how he, as the group's consultant, was to handle that money—investors involved in the plan all knew that Hofman would be depositing the money into a savings account under his own name. One fifth of the money was to be invested in each of five investment options—"speculative mining issues, warrants, industrials, space and research issues…[and finally], 'special opportunities'"—as Hofman saw fit. Binne and his fellow investors were expected to participate in the club for a predetermined length of time before they would be able to withdraw their money and whatever equity it may have gained.

Hofman presented all five investors with the guidelines he'd established—guidelines that allegedly gave him almost absolute power as the administrator of the group's money—and each of the five signed, agreeing with his proposal. It must have seemed like a good idea at the time. Hofman had already been purchasing "penny stocks" on the VSE. But as Binne got to know the investment advisor better, he found he didn't like the way Hofman did business. Three months after his predetermined investment period ended, Binne asked for his money back. In 1994, roughly 30 years after the group had been established and when Binne spoke to reporters about Hofman, Binne had yet to receive the money.

Still, despite Binne's suspicions about Hofman, the hard evidence required to do more than raise a few eyebrows just wasn't there when he first reported his concerns over Hofman's business ethics to the BC Securities Commission. In fact, Binne felt that if there was any suspicion at all from the various watchdogs whose job it was to protect investor money from unsavoury business transactions, it was raised against him. It appeared that Hofman's charisma left those who knew him—personal acquaintances and professional colleagues alike—in disbelief; the "affable" Hofman simply couldn't be anything other than the kind and generous man he portrayed himself to be. Feeling pressured, whether real or imagined, Binne backed away from forcing the issue any further. That meant Hofman was free, at least for the time being, to continue to conduct his business in his own unique way.

It would be another 20 years before another complaint eventually led to anything remotely close to public scrutiny or a cursory reprimand of Hofman, but by then he'd acquired a lot of clients, some of whom were smarting from the experience of having known and trusted the man.

It all sounded good—maybe even a little too good to be true. But Hofman had a way with words; he made his financial propositions sound so reasonable. From January 1986 to March 1991, the investment advisor offered members of his Dutch Canadian community, which included family members and close friends from his church, a deal most couldn't refuse. The well-groomed, well-spoken individual with connections to important people promised his clients a sizeable return of 15 percent or more on investments he would make by trading in U.S. Treasury Bills. Even better, according to reports from the *Vancouver Sun*, Hofman allegedly advised his clients that the investment income would be tax-free. There was one stipulation, though—the money couldn't flow through a Canadian bank.

To an unschooled investor, Hofman's proposal appeared to be as sound as any other. After all, investing money always involved risks, especially the volumes of money that Hofman reputedly preferred to work with. To his way of thinking, a "small investor" was someone who wanted to invest less than $100,000, and he usually told potential clients that he wasn't interested in working with what he considered almost insignificant sums of money. But with a little encouragement, Hofman usually relented and made a show of begrudgingly adding this new, "small" client to his portfolio while repeatedly stressing that he was doing the client a "big favour." Over the years, Hofman had established a reputation for being a man of considerable knowledge and importance in the finance industry, and those who knew him appeared to feel privileged to be able to avail themselves of his expertise.

Adriana and Peter Kersbergen believed in the opportunities for making money that Hofman presented. The Dutch couple had lived through the horrors of World War II before immigrating to Canada and starting a new life. They worked hard, eventually bought a home and looked forward to their golden years with expectation and excitement. When Hofman approached the Kersbergens with the opportunity to invest the $257,000 proceeds from the sale of their home in a short-term investment that promised large returns, the couple took him at his word. The seniors were just a few of many in a similar life situation who were tantalized by Hofman's propositions—and who eventually lost their homes and all their retirement savings in the process.

Years later, reporters in British Columbia, and eventually journalists around the world, published a steady stream of stories about how Hofman's alleged business practices left many families bereft of their entire life savings. Even members of Hofman's own family charged that they'd lost money with him—$1.6 million worth, according to the legal action filed against Hofman in the Supreme Court of BC. It became increasingly clear that Hofman and his Canadian companies, Braman Management Ltd. and Juliana Investments Ltd., hadn't followed through on the majority of their promises. In fact, it was beginning to look as if the cunning businessman never had any intention of doing so in the first place.

The news stories did more than inform a wary public about a possible wolf in their midst; they raised questions about how Hofman had managed to fly under the radar for the bulk of his career in this country, escaping the suspicion of both his professional peers and his trusting clients. One report suggested that Hofman's files held at least one part of the key to his success as a con man. It unveiled Hofman's lack of documentation to back the investment and management services he advertised—there wasn't a lot of paperwork to support the business transactions he allegedly made. There was also the embarrassment that some clients felt over having been taken advantage of by their friend, whereas others were disconcerted because they recognized they'd been careless on their part, neglecting to request regular statements. And in some cases, clients were simply in denial that Hofman had done anything wrong, believing it was all just a big misunderstanding.

Although a surprising few approached Hofman with questions about their investments—it was estimated that only 12 to 16 percent of his clients wanted to move funds in and out of their accounts and were even remotely aware of any problems with their investments—eventually someone was bound to ask questions about what was going on with his or her money. And when Hofman couldn't provide satisfactory answers to the queries brought forward by his more inquisitive investors, it was enough to raise suspicion. Finally, Binne and the odd disgruntled client approaching the "powers that be" weren't alone in their concerns. By the early 1980s, complaints were starting to trickle into the offices of the Certified General Accountants Association of BC (CGA-BC) and other securities watchdogs.

Whenever the CGA-BC or any other regulatory agency is informed of a potential problem with one of its members, an investigation immediately takes place. If some merit to the concern is discovered, the individual in question can be fined, his or her professional status revoked or he or she can be prohibited from performing any kind of investment practices altogether. The complaints issued against Hofman prior to 1986, and until his eventual disappearance in 1991, resulted in several actions. In 1982, Hofman received a two-week suspension from the organization, and in 1987, he was fined $1000. Also in 1987, the Superintendent of Brokers ruled that Hofman "cease trading...in any securities held by or on behalf of any person or entity who has given Braman, Hofman...discretionary authority to make investment decisions on his or its behalf..." Clearly, the professional associations that Hofman belonged to weren't always comfortable with his management practices.

Around the same time, the BC Securities Commission also fined Hofman $50,000 after attempts to prosecute him for a number of "infractions" fell through when they didn't receive enough support from his clients. On another occasion, the investor was reprimanded for trading without a licence. In 1989, Hofman was barred from trading on the VSE. And in 1990, the CGA-BC demanded that he surrender his CGA certificate. Although Hofman had pulled the wool over the eyes of many of his clients, not everyone was buying his "affable" demeanour, and on January 15, 1990, he voluntarily resigned from the CGA-BC. He did, however, make a deal in the process—the CGA-BC agreed to refrain from making Hofman's resignation public.

Clearly, by 1991, when the complaints against Hofman were forwarded to the RCMP's commercial fraud section, the investor had collected several significant hand-slaps from associations like the CGA-BC. There was enough consternation about the man that by April 1991, the police were hot on Hofman's trail. In fact, media reports revealed that he had been under investigation for the better part of a year. At this point, allegations against the businessman were uniformly being considered to be of a criminal nature, and investigators were working with the theory that he operated what analysts believed was a Ponzi scheme.

The Ponzi scheme that Hofman was allegedly operating appeared to be fairly straightforward. Authorities believed that he had been living off the investment money he received from new clients or from the earnings he collected from any successful investments he might have made along the way. It had already been established that, for the most part, Hofman's clients were oblivious to possible problems with their investments and weren't overly demanding in asking for statements or cashing in on their investments. But every now and then, a persistent and perhaps suspicious investor would confront him and insist on getting his or her money back. Hofman was then forced to use some of the money he'd received from new investors to pay off that request and stave off any further suspicion.

This method of deflecting concern worked for quite some time; Hofman was pretty good at damage control and had done so effectively for many years. But the fog of suspicion surrounding him was thickening, and it became clear that the only way he could avoid any further scrutiny was to stop what he was doing. But Hofman wasn't about to do that. Pulling out of the industry would mean he would have to pay off his clients, and he didn't have the money. There was only one thing he could do—continue on as he always had. Despite the RCMP being involved in Hofman's case and his professional activities being forcibly curtailed, the crooked investor proceeded full-steam ahead.

At the same time, Hofman couldn't avoid the hounds at his heels forever. Feeling the mounting pressure, he decided to get away for a while, and in April 1991, he boarded a flight to Amsterdam via Seattle, Washington, on Martinair Canada. That's the last time that anyone, including most of his family members, admits to seeing him. From that moment on, Hofman's associates in Canada say they lost track of the man. It seemed as though Hofman had vanished from the face of the earth.

Investigators grilled family members and acquaintances alike, digging for information about the last interaction any of them might have had with him, but no one admitted to knowing anything about his whereabouts. For a number of investors whose collective losses allegedly reached several millions of dollars, Hofman's disappearance was life altering. A few of those people had the means to bounce back to some degree, but many others lost their investments and it was likely that they'd never see any of that money again.

While his clients struggled with their new financial realities, Hofman was breathing a sigh of relief. By the summer of

1991, he probably thought he was home free. But he had another think coming. Memories run long when it comes to money, and forgiveness, even in the Christian community Hofman purportedly loved, didn't preclude the need to right one's wrongs. If there was any justice in the world, Hofman would be held accountable sooner or later. If that didn't happen during his lifetime, he would find himself making his amends to a much higher court.

A few months after his arrival in Amsterdam, Fred Siebolt Hofman was once again on the move. He straightened his trousers and patted down a few errant hairs on his head as he disembarked the plane he'd just arrived on and made his way to Australian customs. After a cursory check to determine that his visa was in order, the 54-year-old businessman walked into his new life. He was looking forward to starting out fresh in "the land down under."

It's not altogether clear when Hofman started going by the name of Piet Cornelius Walters. If he had travelled to Australia under his birth name, he would have been identified and taken into custody immediately. After all, the Canadian authorities were well aware that Hofman had a daughter living in Australia, so the likelihood that he would make that country his destination instead of returning to the Netherlands wasn't out of the question. Still, sources suggest that Hofman changed his name to Walters some time after his Australian visa expired.

Once he found a new home and secured a few business contacts, Hofman opened a three-branch accounting and financial service called Drury Management Pty. Ltd. and began plying his trade in a place where nobody knew his real name. Of course, being a newcomer does have its drawbacks. Anonymity meant that he had to build a new reputation. But for a man with a flair for the dramatic and a story for everything, this didn't appear to pose much of a problem. Walters, alias Hofman, tackled the task of creating an entirely new backstory with vigour, professing ties to Dutch royalty as the son of the late Prince Bernhard of the Netherlands.

In time, Walters married Virginia Ransom, and in 2000, the couple purchased the Longford Mansion, one of Tasmania's first colonial homes, for a staggering $730,000. Clearly, Hofman didn't share the money problems many of his former investors were experiencing at that time. It was equally clear that the man had effectively recreated himself. But you can only snub your nose at authority for so long, and most who knew Hofman/Walters and his many schemes would have agreed it was about time for the con man's luck to run out.

By 2003, Hofman had effectively woven himself into the social fabric of Australian culture. He'd been equally successful in re-establishing what appeared to be a fairly successful investment practice. Even to the Aussies, Hofman's demeanour was considered affable, and the man masquerading as a prince's son was the centre of high society. But that didn't prevent Australian authorities from arresting him for "immigration irregularities" in April of that year. It appeared that Hofman/Walters had continued to live in his adopted country long after his temporary visa expired.

But that wasn't the original reason he was being investigated. Rolling back the calendar to September 2002, the Australian Securities and Investment Commission (ASIC) had already started a civil action against Walters, alleging that he had "engaged in dishonest conduct in the advice he gave to an investor [about] the establishment of a self-managed superannuation fund, and the subsequent investment of the fund's assets with Drury Management Pty. Ltd." between May 26, 2002, and July 16, 2002.

The ASIC alleged that Walters, his business partner Mark Samuel Evans and Drury Management Pty. Ltd. had obtained loans totalling almost $8 million in Australian currency from about 118 clients scattered between offices in Melanda, Cairns and Atherthon to invest on their behalf. They had also guaranteed a 13.5 percent return on the unsecured investments. The pair was ordered to surrender their passports and "received an interim injunction restraining them from further operating the scheme, receiving or soliciting funds, removing any assets from Australia, or disposing them." On April 15, 2003, a criminal charge followed from the initial civil proceedings, and Hofman was arrested for engaging in "dishonest conduct in relation to the provision of a financial service."

Hofman was 66 years old when he spent his first night in jail waiting to hear the specifics surrounding the charges. It would be the first of many nights to come.

∽

Although several years had passed between Hofman's alleged venture into the world of Ponzi schemes in Canada and the time he was finally identified and apprehended in Australia, it looked as if he'd continued where he'd left off, having secured a footing in the financial world Down Under. The ASIC's allegations against Hofman sounded eerily similar to what he'd been accused of doing in BC.

But not everyone back in Canada was completely upfront with the RCMP during its investigation of the man. According to the stories that emerged shortly after Hofman's arrest in Australia, the one-time investment advisor's schemes were discovered after Ian D. Jessup was appointed as interim receiver, and his investigation traced a $3-million transaction to a "junior brokerage firm in Vancouver" with ties to Raymond Hofman, the missing man's eldest son. While it's not clear what, if any, ramifications this transaction had on Hofman's son, the discovery helped officials make the connection between Hofman and Walters, inevitably leading to the arrest of the former investment counsellor.

It also opened the door to further investigations into the man's actions and a lengthy list of charges being brought against him. On September 16, 2006, after a three-week trial, Hofman was found guilty of "14 charges of dishonesty in relation to the provision of financial services to clients of Drury Management Pty. Ltd." and sentenced to eight years in prison. According to an article in *Money Management,* Hofman's case involved "more than $972,000 belonging to 10 clients."

Of course, being found guilty in a court of law is rarely the end of any most wanted story. Hofman continued to declare his innocence and immediately appealed his conviction. In April 2007, his appeal was granted after his lawyers effectively argued that a sick juror had to leave the deliberation room for more than an hour. Hofman was scheduled for retrial in the fall of 2007. Was it possible that Hofman would get away with his dishonest antics once again?

Of course, the Canadian authorities were still trying to get their hands on the wayward investor. By 2007, the RCMP had charged Hofman with 26 counts of theft and 25 counts of fraud. Depending on the source, and taking into consideration that many of Hofman's Canadian clients never came forward to make a claim, it was estimated that Hofman could have swindled as much as $20 million from them. In order to take Hofman to trial on any of these charges, Canadian authorities needed to get the man back on Canadian soil.

In July 2007, Hofman finally consented to the extradition. However, before the justice system in this country had a chance to get their hooks into the alleged con man, there was a little matter of an Australian retrial to wait for. After almost 20 years, by the time the snow fell on the prairies, Hofman's victims would finally have their day in court.

Of course, like any well-made television drama, Hofman's story would have a few more twists and turns before the Aussies were finished with him.

On November 7, 2007, the *Windmill*, a Dutch North American newspaper, published the following headline: "Hofman Unexpectedly Abandons his Appeal by Pleading Guilty to Fraud, Dutch Canadian to be Resentenced in Australia." At the age of 72, Hofman's years of fighting the authorities had finally broken the man, or perhaps he was stricken with an attack of conscience. In either case, with the Canadians still wanting to get their pound of flesh, Hofman had to know that even if he by some remote chance won his case in Australia, he would still have a lengthy legal battle to fight when the authorities shipped him off to Canada—something that would happen almost immediately with an extradition order in place. There was also the matter of the Dutch authorities in the Netherlands who were reportedly interested in having a face-to-face with Hofman themselves—falsely claiming kinship to the royal family isn't something any country looks kindly upon.

No, perhaps staying put in Australia was about all Hofman could handle—at least for the time being. But by November 2009, just two years into an eight-year sentence, Hofman applied for parole and hoped he'd seen the last of the Capricornia Correctional Centre in Rockhampton, Queensland. Hofman's victims were devastated by the possibility. Kay Anderson was just one of the former investors to step up and speak out against the early release. Anderson told Henry Tettiett of the *Cairns Post* that Hofman was allowed to "come into a community and do what he did to other people and he gets off lightly compared to what investors have had to endure as a consequence of his actions.... People have lost their homes, their livelihoods, their superannuation, their life savings, their business, their relationships and their prospect of a secure future. It has been a pretty hard road for a lot of people, and a lot of those people have not recovered from it." Hofman was denied early parole.

To date, Hofman is biding his time in an Australian prison and has yet to appear in a Canadian court. He remains one of our country's most wanted fugitives.

Part Two

CASE CLOSED

~

For many of us, the most gratifying part of any story, real or imagined, is when the good guys overcome evil, real or perceived, and the perpetrators are punished for their misdeeds. This couldn't be truer than when we've been living with a criminal in our midst, and the authorities finally track that person down.

Public support is often a key ingredient in the speedy capture of a criminal. After the brutal murder of his six-year-old son, Adam, John Walsh made it his personal mission to educate the general public about fugitives who are on the lam and encourage people to come forward with any information they might have. Shows such as *America's Most Wanted*, which debuted in 1988, and newer platforms like *48 Hours Mystery*, have kept the names and faces of criminals at large fresh in the minds of the public. At the time of this writing, *America's Most Wanted* reported 1132 fugitives captured worldwide, thanks, in part, to the tips received after a story about one of these criminals aired.

In Canada, we don't hear as much about our most wanted fugitives as our neighbours to the south might, but they exist nonetheless. Local news stations air mug shots and brief descriptions of the most wanted criminals in their service areas. And thankfully, this partnership between the police and the public has produced positive results.

Killers such as Allan Legere, nicknamed the "Monster of Miramichi," who terrorized an entire region when he was painting the community red with the blood of his victims, are locked away in Canada's most secure prison. Child molester Richard Steve Goldberg finally landed behind bars when a concerned citizen called the police. This section heralds the hard work of our law enforcement personnel with a look at the successful resolutions to some of their most difficult cases.

Machine Gun Molly
Monique Proietti

~

> *We were used to gunmen. We weren't used to a gun woman. That added a whole romantic aura, a new dimension to the story.*
>
> –Veteran crime reporter Michel Auger, to Alan Hustak of the *Montréal Gazette*

Some people would argue that they were born into a life of crime. Others might suggest they'd had it thrust upon them. Both applied in the case of Monique (Monica) Proietti.

To all outward appearances, Monique—a waif-like coquette who barely reached 5 feet in height on a good day and, with the exception of her pregnancies, weighed less than 100 pounds—looked every part the lady. A stranger watching her push her pram down one of Montréal's northend streets might describe her as a doting mother, strict even, when her errant toddler did something displeasing. They'd likely never use the adjectives "threatening," "domineering" or "cunning" to describe her persona.

Machine Gun Molly
Monique Proietti

Those same strangers would soon learn that looks are indeed deceiving, and that Monique was a master of deception.

Childcare specialists speak about risk factors when dealing with youth who stray from making healthy life choices and veer into delinquency. Children who grow up in an unstable environment where they are challenged by difficult situations are often in danger of developing dysfunctional lifestyles themselves. Such risk factors include absent or negligent parents and parents with substance abuse issues. As well, children who experience some kind of extreme trauma and don't get the help they need to process that trauma in a healthy way are considered to be at risk.

As a little girl, Monique had more strikes against her than many other high-risk children. She made her grand entry into this world in 1939, one of eight children born to a poor family living in a corner of Montréal's "red-light district." Ironically, one Montréal travel website states that the area earned that moniker after it was established as a "necessary evil to protect innocent girls from the dangers of lusty sailors." Yet, from a very young age, Monique was primed for just such a purpose, and the person grooming her for a life of prostitution and crime was none other than her own grandmother.

Monique's grandmother, Maria, was accused of teaching young, impressionable children the ins and outs of life on the wrong side of the law. Even more disturbing, young girls who came her way were allegedly schooled in the life of the "working girl." And although sources don't suggest she ever faced charges stemming from those accusations, she was charged with and found guilty of receiving stolen goods. At the age of 60, Maria was looking at spending a goodly portion of her golden years in the Kingston Prison for Women after being handed a 12-year sentence.

It appears that Monique was a good student; at least she learned the lessons her grandmother taught her well. Some sources suggest that the young girl began plying her trade at the tender age of 13 in order to help support her impoverished family, and that she quit school in the fifth grade to focus more of her energies on her growing interest in a life of crime.

By 1956, she was no longer sweet and had definitely been kissed a time or two, but it appeared she had decided to settle down somewhat. She was 17 when she met and married a 33-year-old Scottish gangster named Anthony Smith, and during their relatively short marriage, the couple produced two children. But in 1962, Smith was deported from Canada to the UK, having illegally overstayed his welcome in this country and leaving Monique behind to provide for herself and her children with her somewhat limited education and resources.

During her short time with Smith, Monique experienced a horrific family tragedy that only added to the sad tale that was her life. When she was 19 years old, the aging tenement building her family lived in burned to the ground, killing her mother, a sister and three brothers in the blazing inferno, and severely injuring several other members of her family. One sister spent two years in hospital recovering from third-degree burns to over half her body.

Although Monique didn't experience the fire firsthand, her family's tragedy weighed heavily on her. But the grief of burying half her family members and watching others she loved suffer through unimaginable pain also toughened Monique's personal resolve. That she was strengthened through her trials was probably a good thing; she still had a long line of losses in store. A brief relationship with another bad boy, Viateur Tessier, produced a third child, but the relationship ended when he was incarcerated for armed robbery in 1966.

It was becoming increasingly clear that Monique couldn't really count on the men in her life for any kind of support. If she wanted to ensure a quality of life for herself and her children, she'd have to take matters into her own hands.

It was the summer of 1967. While an estimated 50 million visitors basked in the thrill of the 1967 International and Universal Exposition held in Montréal from April 27 to October 29, Monique's life was looking bleak. At that point, with three hungry youngsters depending on her and no means to meet their needs, Monique put some of her grandmother's lessons to good use. After handpicking the men she'd lead on an unprecedented crime spree, she organized a plan of attack. She promised herself that if she and her team of marauders hit enough banks over the next few weeks or months and brought in a sufficient amount of cash, she would pack up her children and head south to Florida and leave the sordid life of crime behind.

Of course, robbing banks is anything but a safe proposition. Reminiscing about his time on Toronto's crime beat, journalist Jocko Thomas told reporter Joe Warmington that until 1960, most of the bank tellers were men, and most of them packed a gun. "In fact, down at King and Bay, under the old banks, there was a firing range where they used to practice," Thomas explained. By 1967, bringing a gun to work was no longer the norm, but the staff still remembered those days, and a shootout with bank robbers was always a possibility.

With a flair for the theatrical, Monique would don one of her bleach-blonde wigs and dark glasses or pump up the makeup and pull a large, dark hood over her head whenever she went out to "work." It didn't take long before the witnesses of these heists noticed there was a woman involved and that she appeared to be calling the shots. Once the media got hold of the fact that the rash of bank robberies sweeping the city was being masterminded by a member of the fairer sex, Monique's legend grew. The story was just too unbelievable.

Long before her identity was ever confirmed, Monique had earned the title "Machine Gun Molly," a moniker credited to *Montréal Star* writer Tim Burke. Although the police didn't know her real name, she was a wanted woman running on borrowed time. The media had a field day, pumping out reams of copy on the story. Tales of her taking her children on a heist to allegedly distract any suspicion being cast her way, her habit of giving money to the poor, and her ability to wield a machine gun during bank robberies astonished the community. And even when someone suggested there were flaws in some of those stories, the claims went unnoticed. Residents lapped up the Hollywood feel of the saga; even Monique reportedly loved reading the news clips highlighting her latest exploits. And although the bank robberies weren't taken lightly by anyone, some people actually rooted for Machine Gun Molly and hoped for a happy ending to her story. After all, the woman's actions might have threatened violence, but no one was ever hurt during any of her heists.

Despite the differences of opinion over Machine Gun Molly and her gang, one thing was eminently clear—with 19 successful bank robberies under her belt, Monique had earned herself the reputation as "Montréal's most famous female gangster." One more go-round was all she wanted.

She should have quit while she was ahead.

⌘

Machine Gun Molly's 20th heist would be her last. She was determined to follow through with her plans to move to Florida. She just needed a little more cash, padding for her nest egg in case of emergencies.

At around 11 o'clock on the morning of Tuesday, September 19, 1967, Monique and her boys pulled into the Caisse Populaire in St. Vital, Montréal-Nord. She wore a hooded jacket pulled low over her head as she and her two partners entered the building. An article in *La Presse*, dated the same day as the heist, describes how the three robbers held up the bank and made away with around $3000.

A quick exit is always the key to any successful bank robbery, and once they had emptied two drawers, Molly and her gang rushed out of the bank and into a Chrysler parked outside. Of course, as soon as the trio fled, the police were called and reportedly arrived on the scene within 30 seconds.

The authorities' quick response as well as an accurate description of the getaway vehicle meant police had no trouble honing in on the robbers. A high-speed chase ensued between officers and the brazen bandits, weaving through the streets of Montréal-Nord and Saint-Michel at speeds of up to 160 kilometres per hour. At one point in the pursuit, the three suspects ditched their Chrysler and absconded with another vehicle. The chase ended when the car Monique was riding in collided with a bus. Her two partners fled the scene, leaving Machine Gun Molly to face the music alone.

Only a handful of people know what really happened in those last moments when Monique and the officers came face to face. She would have known that her run of fame and fortune had come to an end, that the dream of moving to Florida would never become a reality and that the curtain was about to fall on this drama. But it is difficult to believe that this woman, who to that point hadn't shown herself to be particularly violent, would have pulled a .45-calibre gun on the police—unless, perhaps, she was hoping to commit suicide via cop.

Newspaper accounts of Monique's last moments explain that the police at the scene thought the elusive crime boss wouldn't hesitate to shoot, and officers didn't give her a chance to pull the trigger. At the age of 27, Machine Gun Molly lay dead in a Montréal street from gunshot wounds to the head and chest. The glamorous queen of crime was no more.

Although the authorities might have suspected that Monique was the woman behind the robberies, she was never charged or publicly named as a person of interest in any of the 20 bank heists that blanketed Montréal during that hot summer of 1967. She had a court date, however, on October 6 on a charge of vehicle theft laid by Jacques-Cartier police. Perhaps that was the authorities' way of keeping tabs on the woman they secretly believed was Machine Gun Molly? After all, the officials were aware of the Proietti family and the exploits of some of its members. Although he no longer lives a life of crime, Mario, one of Monique's brothers, was once reputed to have made a comfortable living for himself when he was "in the business," so to speak.

Mario suggested to Georges-Hebert Germain, the author of *Souvenirs de Monica*, a biography of Machine Gun Molly, that with the exception of Monique's daughter, Ginette, the majority of his family weren't "legits"—people with jobs and homes and normal families. In short, the Proietti name was known to law enforcement of the day.

It could have been the tragic life Monique was born into that stirred compassion among the people who read of her exploits. She never really had much of a chance at a normal life; poverty can be paralyzing for the people who live it day in and day out. At the same time, Monique's children were born into pretty much the same situation as their mother. And when Monique was killed, her children's lives continued to deteriorate. Ginette was only eight years old when her mother died, and for a long time, she wouldn't accept that reality, choosing instead to believe that her mother was in hiding and would return to Ginette and her brothers when it was safe. Of course, Monique never returned, and Ginette and Tony, the two children Monique had with Smith, were sent to live with their father in England.

Although she remembers her childhood as being "terrible," and Ginette started her own adult life with the significant challenge of being a single mother, she struggled to make healthier decisions than her parents had. Germain's book, a partially fictionalized account of Monique's life, is told through Ginette's perspective, and while it hasn't been easy, Ginette has managed to make it "through to the side of the 'legits,'" as Mario describes them.

But her life is an ongoing struggle, and Ginette will likely spend a considerable portion of it healing the scars of her dysfunctional childhood. As she told Janet Bagnall of the *Montréal Gazette*, "What happened to me is what happens to the children of criminals…It's the children who pay."

The same was true for her mother.

Since Machine Gun Molly's death, stories about the crime boss have varied depending on the people telling them and the motives behind their words. Tales of the woman's exploits were still being told 11 years after her death, when Ginette returned to Montréal from England.

While some folks still thought Monique was a folk hero—a female Robin Hood of sorts, stealing from the rich and sharing the spoils with anyone in need—other opinions about the woman weren't as kind. A *CTV News* story broadcast in May 2004 featured Monique's sister, Rita, saying her sister "had become dangerous," and that she was glad the police killed her.

Glamorous gangster, tragic heroine, cold-hearted crime boss—probably all of these terms apply to varying degrees when describing Machine Gun Molly and her wild exploits. What is certain and can go down in history as fact and not just opinion, was that Monique was a leader with enough charisma to motivate the men in her charge to pull off 20 armed robberies that netted the group in excess of $100,000. And she died in a hail of bullets on a cold Montréal street on September 19, 1967, with the furor of Expo still in full swing.

Cover Girl Bandit
Christine Bartlett

I wondered, oh God, will I see my family for Christmas or (will they) come to my workplace and see me in a puddle of blood.

–Melissa Dato, *Toronto Star,* June 14, 2008

Formed in 1974, the bustling city of Mississauga might still be a newbie as far as large Canadian centres go, but in 2010 it was recognized as our country's sixth largest and fastest growing major city. About 729,000 residents called Mississauga home at that point in its history, many of whom were drawn to the city because of its blend of natural beauty and economic strength—according to its website, the city is home to "61 Fortune 500 Canadian or major divisional head offices and 50 Fortune Global 500 Canadian headquarters."

Flagging itself as the "safest city in Canada eight years in a row" is another powerful drawing card for some folks. People like to know that they live and work in a safe environment. They shouldn't be scared to leave their homes and conduct their daily business, regardless where that business might take them.

Melissa Dato certainly wasn't worried about anything untoward happening when she left her home on the morning of Christmas Eve 2007. The TD Canada Trust branch where she worked as a teller, on Burnhamthorpe Road in Mississauga, closed early that day—early enough for her to put the final touches on her Christmas preparations and really begin to look forward to the season's festivities. She probably didn't bat an eyelash when a youngish-looking woman walked into the bank all bundled up in winter wear and took her place in line. While the weather at that time of year in Mississauga is a lot milder than other parts of the country, temperatures can hover around freezing. Combine that with the cool, damp air masses floating in from Lake Ontario, and it's understandable that some residents would add a few layers to keep the chill out.

Of course, in retrospect, you might concede that it was a bit odd when the woman didn't remove the dark scarf wrapped around her mouth or pull off her gloves when she approached the teller. A person might have been a tad concerned when instead of speaking, the woman handed the teller a handwritten note. But remember, this was the safest city in the country, and even though Dato worked in a bank, when was the last time a teller had to worry about workplace safety?

Most Canadians aren't aware of the various crime figures Statistics Canada collects on a regular basis, but if they were, chances are they'd know that generally speaking, you're more likely to have your home burglarized or to get mugged on the street than experience a bank robbery. In fact, statistics from 2004 state that only five percent of the robberies in Canada occurred in a bank—the days of hold-'em-up-an'-shoot-'em-out bank heists are most certainly a thing of the past. No one would dare pull off a bank job in this "safest city." And a bank robbery on Christmas Eve was the last thing anyone at TD Canada Trust expected.

However, if you are a newsy sort of person who follows current events, you might remember that by December 24, 2007, Mississauga had experienced a rash of bank robberies.

Noon on November 10, 2007. The Bank of Montréal at Cawthra Road and Burnhamthorpe Road East. A woman with a plastic bag and a note walks into the branch and approaches the first available teller. Her silence may have been a little disconcerting to the teller serving her, but that consternation soon evolved into fear as the teller unfolded the paper and read the words on the note. The woman's note said that she had a gun and instructed the teller to "put all the money in the bag or die."

The entire scene seemed so incredulous. A bad dream. Who robs banks these days? Especially women? Machine Gun Molly had been a pretty notorious character in Montréal, but that was decades earlier. And Molly was certainly a one-of-a-kind, anyway. Things like that don't happen every day...

Then again.

A nervous energy rushed through the teller's body as she grabbed the money from her till. The woman with the scarf wrapped around her face and a heavy coat covering her upper body took the cash the teller handed her and left the bank. It was a simple as that. No hoopla. No guns blazing. No sirens—at least until the woman left and the bank alerted the authorities.

If anyone thought that the police arriving at the scene would manage a quick arrest, they had another thought coming. The woman disappeared into the street crowds as inconspicuously as she'd entered the bank. The teller couldn't provide a clear description of the robber, aside from estimating that she was around 5-feet-5 or 5-feet-6 inches tall and weighed between 140 and 160 pounds. Even the bank's surveillance video wasn't very helpful in offering up any distinctive characteristics that might help to identify the woman. And to add to the air of mystery surrounding the bank robber, the police could find no connection between the November 10 incident and any other similar crime in the city's recent history, or even in neighbouring districts. It was inconceivable, but the robber might just get away with her brazen act.

Cover Girl Bandit
Christine Bartlett

There's a funny thing about human nature. Once we do something naughty and manage to get away with it, we find ourselves compelled to do it again—just ask anyone who has ever committed an act of infidelity. It wasn't surprising, then, that once the adrenalin had worn off from her first attempt, the woman who'd made off with an undisclosed amount of money decided to ply her newfound skills once again.

Exactly two weeks later, at around 8:22 on the morning of November 24, the Dundas Street branch of the TD Canada Trust received a visit from a woman matching the same description as the one who had robbed the Bank of Montréal. Looking back, bank officials might have scolded themselves for not noticing the woman until it was too late and another teller's drawer had been emptied. There was absolutely no variation between the way this new heist was committed and the robbery on November 10. A middle-aged woman—at least they thought it was a woman—of average build bundled in a dark coat, dark scarf and dark gloves handed a note to a teller demanding cash. Just like the previous incident, no identifying features were noted. With no new leads, police likely thought their chances of capturing the woman were decreasing by the minute. It looked as though she was going to get away with robbery…again.

And then the unthinkable happened. On December 5, she struck once more. This time, only 11 days separated this robbery from the former one. She seemed to be gaining confidence with each success.

The police were seriously baffled. Although women do commit bank robberies, it's rare to see the fairer sex committing a string of such acts. The last time a woman repeatedly held up banks in the area was in 1998. The 46-year-old woman in that case was dubbed the "Floppy Hat Bandit," and she completed 10 jobs over the course of 14 months before she was caught. But instead of serving jail time, Linda Michaud, who struggled with depression and a gambling addiction, agreed to get professional help.

The culprit in the Mississauga robberies was now given a handle of her own. Peel Regional Police officers tagged her the "Cover Girl Bandit." If she hadn't captured the attention of Mississauga residents by now, she was about to startle them and the men in blue charged with protecting them even more.

On December 8, just three days after the previous bank robbery, while residents were still digesting the media stories about her most recent heist, the Cover Girl Bandit struck again. That day, her financial institution of choice was the So-Use Credit Union on Bristol Road. She approached a teller with her demands at around 2:00 PM and made off with an undisclosed amount of money. That she continued to rob banks and the increasing frequency with which she was committing her crimes, suggested that the Cover Girl Bandit was becoming more sure of her abilities. And if the authorities thought that Christmas might provide the residents and police officers of Mississauga a little reprieve from her exploits, they were mistaken.

COVER GIRL BANDIT
CHRISTINE BARTLETT

Melissa Dato had barely begun her day's work when the Cover Girl Bandit approached her wicket at 9:00 AM on Christmas Eve. Christine Bartlett, the real name of the Cover Girl Bandit, scored her largest take that morning—Dato handed her $7000 before Bartlett left the bank and disappeared into the Christmas crowds. Dato would later face the brazen robber once again, this time in a court of law while delivering her victim impact statement. Dato explained how her life changed during that altercation, how she really thought she was going to die that day and how, since the robbery, she was constantly nervous and always looked over her shoulder. But before Dato got the chance to tell Bartlett how she felt, the Cover Girl Bandit struck again.

Altogether, Bartlett held up nine banks and two credit unions between November 10, 2007, and March 22, 2008. Nine of the financial institutions were in Mississauga and two were in Oakville, and Bartlett robbed the TD Canada Trust where Dato worked on two separate occasions.

In the end, a joint effort between the public and the police led to the eventual arrest of Christine Bartlett. Repeated showings of video clippings of the Cover Girl Bandit, taken from surveillance footage and aired on prime time newscasts, produced one tip in particular that grabbed the attention of investigators. That tip came from a person who had worked with Bartlett and told police that the woman had frequented homeless shelters. Soon after police received that first bit of information, they learned that Bartlett had signed into one of the area's shelters. She was arrested without incident.

After pulling in more than $30,000 during her tenure as a female bank robber, Bartlett was surprisingly penniless at the time of her arrest. Even more surprising was that until just a few months before she was apprehended, Bartlett had been holding down two jobs and hadn't committed a single criminal act in her life. Although police believed they had their suspect, a lot of questions still needed to be answered.

Christine Bartlett's story, before that fateful November day that altered the course of her life forever, was a typically sad one. The 38-year-old divorced mother of three had been struggling for some time. She'd had what she described as several abusive relationships, one of which led to the sexual abuse of her daughter. Bartlett had dabbled in drugs from time to time to help ease the stresses in her life, but she didn't appear to have an addiction problem. Aside from paying a drug dealer who'd allegedly threatened her partner, and paying some overdue bills as well as having a dinner out, the money she stole was largely unaccounted for. Defence lawyer Peter Scully told *Toronto Star* reporters after Bartlett's trial that "most of the money was turned over to another person."

In light of earlier statements made by Peel Regional Police Detective Marty Pollock, Bartlett's claim seemed true.

"She had absolutely no money on her," Pollock told the media the day after Bartlett's arrest. "Other than basically the clothes on her back, she had absolutely nothing."

It was hard to imagine what tipped the scales in Bartlett's mind and led her to such uncharacteristic behaviour as to pull off the 11 robberies she had been charged with and eventually pleaded guilty to. Despite her tale of woe and the fact that she didn't own or carry a gun and had no intentions of hurting anyone, the Cover Girl Bandit didn't get off as easily as her Floppy Hat predecessor. Justice Katherine McLeod acknowledged Bartlett's troubles and expressed compassion for the clearly disturbed woman, but she was compelled to take into consideration the seriousness of the crimes when determining Bartlett's sentence. In the end, the Cover Girl Bandit received a four-year sentence, which was slightly less than the prosecution's suggestion of five to seven years. McLeod said she had to take into account the woman's threats of violence. After being granted six months' credit for the time she'd spent in custody prior to her trial, Bartlett was looking at serving 42 months of jail time.

Bartlett purportedly cried throughout her two-hour-long sentencing. Before being transported to prison, Bartlett asked to address the court. Amid a flood of tears, she said how sorry she was for her actions.

"I would truly have never harmed you," she told Dato. "I hope you can accept my apology and forgive me."

"I do," Dato replied.

The *American Heritage Dictionary of Idioms* credits the comic strip character Dick Tracy with first using the phrase, "Crime does not pay." Some criminals get away with their illegal exploits for a time, but the law—or karma—eventually catches up with them. In some situations, however, it's hard to see how anything remotely positive might have come out of the quest to make a quick buck illegally.

That certainly was the case for Christine Bartlett.

The Gentleman Bandit
Edwin Alonzo Boyd

Well they tried to fasten the guilt on the people that were related to the ones that I had problems with, but they couldn't prove it so they finally had to drop it. I mean, I was the guilty one, but they were the ones that were in a position to be blamed…the point was that nobody got any problem with it except the people that I had to do away with.

–Edwin Alonzo Boyd, in an interview with the CBC shortly before his death in 2002

Thirty-nine-year-old George Vigus Sr. knew he was going against everything he stood for, but he couldn't help himself. He'd been smitten with 21-year-old Iris Scott ever since he first laid eyes on her at the box factory where he worked. If word of their affair got out, it would destroy his wife, disillusion his kids and devastate his entire family. But after falling in love with Iris, George just couldn't pull away. He was a doomed man.

A man entering his middle years sometimes doesn't feel as youthful and desirable as he once did, and being with Iris renewed George's spirit and made him feel young a little longer. He knew that someday he'd pay dearly for his indiscretion, but he had no idea that "someday" was already upon him.

Officials later speculated that George and Iris were probably enjoying the fresh air in High Park in the fall of 1947, in what was then a secluded part of north Toronto, gazing up at the stars and pushing all their cares away when a man, later identified as Edwin Alonzo Boyd, approached them. The couple must have been immediately concerned since the man was carrying a Luger. He was also wearing gloves and holding what looked like a length of rope.

Some kind of exchange took place between Boyd and the couple that led him to make a snap decision. It was time to use the hand-to-hand combat he'd learned during his war service overseas. He was good at it, he knew. Good enough that he had taught the other men in his unit the commando tactics he'd perfected. Problem was, he'd never had the opportunity to use the skills he'd become so proud of. Here was his chance. As far as he was concerned, this couple was too mouthy for their own good.

"They were strangers to me, but I was out practising," Boyd later confessed. "They were mouthing off what they were going to do, and I decided that it would be better for me to dispatch them."

A coroner's report later stated that George was hit on the forehead and then "garroted with the sash rope." Iris had injuries to her face and wrists. It looked as though she'd been strangled with bare hands—commando style. Boyd then dumped the two dead bodies into the trunk of the 1935 Chevrolet Coupe the couple had arrived in and returned to his own wife and children as if he'd just completed a typical day on the job.

News of the double murder spread throughout Toronto and was the subject of coffee-break chatter for quite some time. Police were initially looking at George's son, George Jr., and his friend, Bill Broadbridge, as possible suspects. Suspicion fell on Bill because he was first on the scene. He and his girlfriend had driven to the area and noticed what looked like an abandoned car. Bill thought he recognized the car as belonging to a family friend, George Vigus Sr. After calling his high school buddy, George Jr., and hearing that his dad appeared to have gone missing, Bill met up with his buddy and the two young men went to the scene together. They also called police, who arrived there at roughly the same time as the boys. Since nothing seemed out of place, the police told George Jr. he could remove the car. Not having planned for that, George Jr. had to return home to pick up the spare set of keys. He also asked his uncle, Lloyd Vigus, to come with him and Bill to collect the vehicle, and when they returned to the park, Lloyd noticed that the trunk was locked. Thinking this was odd, Lloyd used a crowbar and popped the trunk. That's when they discovered the bodies of George Sr. and Iris.

It wasn't until December 1947, when a coroner's jury declared that an "unknown person" was responsible for the brutal slayings, that Bill and George Jr. were officially dismissed as suspects in the case. The case went cold and remained that way for more than half a century.

Toronto was already a bustling city in 1949. The end of the war allowed most people to think more positively about their futures. They no longer had to rely on food ration books. Business was picking up. Newfoundland and Labrador had joined Confederation. Things were generally looking hopeful.

Most of the soldiers who'd served time overseas were anxious to return to the routine of a regular life. Nine-to-five jobs, family suppers and kids clamouring for the attention of their fathers warmed a lot of hearts. But other soldiers found adjusting to civilian life challenging.

Edwin Alonzo Boyd was one of those soldiers who experienced a difficult transition on his return from duty. He had found himself a lovely war bride during his time overseas, and by the time Doreen Boyd sailed for Canada in December 1944, she had three children in tow—one child from a previous marriage and a set of twins with Edwin.

Finding a job after the war didn't seem to pose much of a problem for Edwin Boyd. At one point, he secured steady employment as a streetcar driver with the Toronto Transit

Commission (TTC). However, Boyd didn't feel any connection to the job. It bored him. Life bored him. The real world didn't give him the same kind of thrill he'd found in his fight for survival in the savage battlefields of World War II. And so he quit his job with the TTC and wandered around for a while until pinching pennies got too cumbersome and he had to find another job. That one, too, would eventually bore him, and the cycle would repeat itself.

Looking back, the quest for excitement appeared to course through Boyd's veins from the time he was a young lad. His dad, Glover, was a police officer, a religious man with a stern disposition and a desire for his son to learn to play the violin. Rebelling against his father's wishes and eager to experience the world on his own terms, Boyd left home and became a drifter, hiding out in boxcars and crisscrossing the countryside until he tired of that and decided to try his luck with the army.

Of course, his father had a hand in encouraging his son to enlist. It would be good for the boy, he must have thought. By that time, Glover had watched his son spend three days in jail for a dine-and-dash in 1936 and serve a two-and-a-half-year sentence for robbing a gas station. The senior Boyd had struggled to raise his children alone after Edwin's mother passed away from scarlet fever. Edwin was just 15 at the time and wrestled with his mother's death. Glover had done what he could, trying to raise his children right, but his son's antics wore on him. It was time the boy grew up, and the army was as good a place as any to do that.

After the war, Boyd was back in the same situation where he began when he was living at home—shuffling about trying to make some excitement for himself. Perhaps starting his own business would add a little thrill to the workaday world, he thought. So he started a window-washing company, a job that kept him busy, if not happy, for a while. Stalking through the nights with his Luger in hand and a length of sash rope from his window-washing business over his shoulder, like he was practising for an impending attack, added a bit of daring to his otherwise staid life. It took the edge off his anxiety for a time.

By September 1949, his imaginative romps were getting old. There had to be some way a man could earn a living and live an exciting life. That's when Boyd took a final step in determining the way his future would eventually unfold. One fateful day that month, he stuffed his cheeks with cotton, painted his face with makeup and pulled his trademark fedora onto his head. He then downed a bottle of liquid courage before barging his way into a Bank of Montréal in north Toronto with guns blazing, demanding that the tellers empty their drawers and making off with an estimated $2256 (about $17,000 in today's currency). Dodging the bullets being fired at him from the bank manager's revolver, Boyd made it out safe and sound. He'd successfully carried out his first bank robbery. It was almost as easy as the other thefts he'd committed as a youth. Now that he'd gotten away with robbing a bank, how long, he wondered, would it take before the cops would be on his trail?

His destiny was sealed from that moment on.

Boyd was comfortable in his own skin, confident in his abilities. Some time after the first bank robbery, he decided to test how successful his disguise was and returned to that same Bank of Montréal, strolled up to the teller and asked for change for a $20 bill. No one recognized him without the makeup and flashy moves, and this reinforced his decision to carry on in this new field on a full-time basis.

Boyd didn't initially look for partners to join him in his endeavours. He'd successfully pulled several bank robberies on his own and emerged unscathed from each one. Boyd also liked to add some theatrics to his robberies, hurling himself over the countertops like he was an Olympic gymnast on a pommel horse, smiling at the ladies as he passed by. He was playing a role, really, just like those loveable Hollywood characters did on the big screen. It earned him the reputation of being quite the gentleman when he conducted his business, and an attractive one at that. Debonair even. Working with someone might cramp his style—it also meant he'd be sharing half the take.

On the other hand, not all of his efforts went off without a hitch. There were countless examples of his ineptitude.

During one heist, a bank manager pulled his gun and started firing long before Boyd had the chance to stuff his bag full of bills. Boyd was lucky to make it out alive from that botched attempt. Another time, a bank employee jumped into a car and tried to chase Boyd down.

A partner might shake things up a bit, Boyd was sure, but a partner might also pick up on a few details Boyd missed and smooth out some of the wrinkles in his plans. He eventually hooked up with Howard Gault, a former jail guard, and the two worked together for a time. Gault was every bit as likely to stumble in the commission of his crimes as Boyd. After one heist, it was Gault that police caught up with first. With more than $12,000 stashed on his person, Gault didn't stand a chance pleading not guilty to the robbery, and Boyd was apprehended a short time later, thanks to the information Gault spilled to police during his interrogation. It was off to jail for both men.

That heist landed Boyd in Toronto's Don Jail sometime in mid-October 1951, where he met Lennie Jackson and another gangster, Willie Jackson (although the two shared the same last name, they were not related). Lennie and his partner, Steve Suchan, were career criminals with a reputation for violent heists. Willie also had a history of committing bank robberies, but he was a lighthearted sort who added a bit of levity to the group. A bond quickly formed between Lennie, Willie and Boyd as they worked together on their first great escape.

In those days, guards didn't search artificial limbs for contraband, and Lennie had a wooden foot. In that wooden foot, he had hidden an assortment of hacksaw blades. None of the jail cells where Boyd and his newfound partners were held had windows, but there was a window in the hall on the way to the gallows. The trio had already managed to create a makeshift key that opened their cells. Once out of their cells, Lennie, Willie and Edwin laboured together, hacking through the single barred window, taking turns sawing and standing watch. On November 4, 1951, they sawed their last stroke, broke through the bars and leapt through the window. They then hoisted themselves over the walls surrounding the prison and propelled themselves to freedom by using several bed sheets tied together. The gallant Boyd and his buddies were out of jail. One source said that four hours elapsed before anyone discovered the jailbreak. Authorities were more than a little disturbed by the news, as were the bankers in town, but the daring escape made enthralling copy for Ontario's big city dailies and for newspapers across the country.

After their escape, the three men initially met up with Steve Suchan at a safe house in Cabbagetown. The group split up, with Lennie and his girlfriend going to Montréal, later followed by Suchan, and Boyd and Willie staying in Suchan's family's west-end home. But realizing they'd need money to hole up for any length of time, the four men reconnected and pulled a couple of heists, one of which is still referred to as the largest in Toronto's history. From that point on, Boyd and his buddies were referred to as the "Boyd Gang." Lennie was really the mastermind in the group, but Boyd's good looks and displays of bravado gave him a distinctive quality that tantalized the imagination of an inquiring public.

After their big heist, Boyd and Willie returned to Suchan's father's house to hide out for a while. The old man seemed nice enough. Heck, he even provided the pair with the great idea to stash the money in a wall of the house. The only problem was that the apple doesn't fall far from the tree. Suchan's old man was as crooked as his son—in the morning, Boyd and Willie woke to find their host gone, along with their money. They had no choice but to join their friends in Montréal or maybe pull a few more heists. During their four months on the lam, the Boyd Gang pulled a total of four robberies, netting them an estimated $75,000.

But it's only ever a matter of time before the law catches up with a practising criminal. Willie's luck ran out when the cops pulled him over and discovered he was carrying a gun. Learning his identity, the police returned Willie to Toronto. Hearing of their friend's bad luck, Lennie, Boyd and Suchan also made their respective ways back to Toronto.

It wasn't until March 6, 1952, that all the members of the gang were recaptured and returned to the Don Jail, but not before officer Edmund Tong took a bullet for his efforts. Tong and his partner, Roy Perry, had been following a 1951 Mercury Monarch after receiving a tip that it belonged to members of the Boyd Gang. The officers signalled to the Monarch to pull over, and Tong started to walk toward the vehicle. The officer didn't have a chance to talk to Lenny or Suchan before bullets started flying. Tong was seriously wounded; the bullet entered his chest severing his spinal cord. Perry was still in the police cruiser, and the gunfire was coming his way as well. He managed to get away with a gunshot wound to his arm.

Suchan and Lennie must have known they wouldn't be able to outrun the authorities forever. No one got away with shooting a peace officer. The streets were crawling with police. And if Tong died from his wound, it wouldn't be long before the pair was captured and sentenced to the hangman's noose. Police officials flooded the province, searching everywhere for the men, and even though Boyd hadn't taken part in the shooting, his profile and the fact that he was still at large also made headlines. The police managed to bring in every member of the gang, beginning with Steve Suchan. Police took him down at his own apartment. Lennie Jackson was the next to be captured—it took tear gas to take him in. Edwin Alonzo Boyd and his brother, Norman, were arrested without incident while they were sleeping.

With the Boyd Gang behind bars once again, the police could breathe a sigh of relief. Staff at the Don Jail were probably thrilled, too. On the other hand, they might have been a bit nervous, wondering what a regular workday would look like with the hoodlums back in jail.

And the guards had every reason to be nervous.

Administrators at the Don Jail might have had some concerns about having Boyd and his gang in their institution, but clearly they hadn't put a lot of thought into how to handle the situation when all four prisoners were placed together in the same cellblock. When news emerged that Tong had died from his injuries, it only added to their worries. Before he died, the officer had named Steve Suchan as his shooter. That meant Suchan's charges were upgraded to murder, and Lennie was now an accomplice in Tong's death. Neither man had anything to lose. Together with Willie and Boyd, who weren't overly enamoured with the idea of spending the rest of their lives in a one-by-three-metre cell barely wide enough for a prisoner to squeeze onto his cot, Lennie and Suchan began planning their second escape from prison.

Boyd and his buddies worked on making another key so they could escape from their cells and saw through another set of bars. They'd managed to get an impression of the key when Willie grabbed it from one of the guards and pretended to lock Suchan's cell. While he had the key in his hands, Willie squeezed hard, leaving a slight impression of the key on his palm before handing it back to the guard. Although Lennie's wooden foot was likely checked for contraband, Willie talked one of their lawyers into smuggling in a hacksaw blade and a piece of metal. Once the key was replicated, the four men arranged to leave their cells for 30 minutes a day during the time the guards were busy supervising prisoner transfers. On September 7, barely six months after being recaptured and one day before Suchan and Jackson's trial was set to begin, the four broke free.

The backlash from their escape was far more damning for the authorities than the gang's first getaway, and with four convicts on the loose, it should have been. The prison warden and several guards were suspended following the incident. Once again, police were engaged in a manhunt of mammoth proportions. And if anyone felt any support for the escapees, it soon dissipated when police offered a $26,000 reward for information on the whereabouts of the convicts leading to an arrest.

Money talks every time. Everyone wanted to get in on the action. Calls came into police headquarters from as far away as North Bay, Ontario. Surprisingly, information from a local tipster, who reported seeing the men in North York, just 24 kilometres from the Don Jail, led to the gang's capture. Police wasted no time getting to the scene, and soon all four members of the Boyd Gang were back in jail where they belonged. It was the last time prison officials would allow the slimy gangsters to slip away on them.

Steve Suchan and Lennie Jackson were almost immediately tried and found guilty of Tong's murder. They were sentenced to die on December 16, 1952, and the pair met the hangman's noose shortly after midnight. Willie was sentenced to 20 years for his crimes, and Boyd received eight life sentences—one for every bank robbery he admitted to pulling.

Willie was released from jail after serving 14 years of his sentence. Boyd was paroled in 1966 but was returned to jail for parole violations. He was incarcerated in the Kingston Penitentiary for another four years before his final release. It was during his time in Kingston that Boyd connected with the Bible and changed his ways for good. Aside from two attempts to escape by sawing through prison bars, Boyd was considered a "model prisoner."

It appears that living a normal life had gained new appeal for Boyd, who settled down in British Columbia under the name of John McCallum after he was released from prison. Boyd and his wife, Doreen, divorced in 1970, and Boyd took a job driving a bus for disabled people. The one-time gangster eventually remarried, having fallen in love with Marjorie, a disabled woman he met while driving the bus. The two spent the better part of the next three decades together, with Boyd serving as her primary caregiver as well as her doting husband. He also took on the responsibility of caring for one of Marjorie's friends, Pear Hall. At one time, Boyd told reporters that caring for the two physically challenged women, who were both confined to wheelchairs, was his "penance," but he would never elaborate on what he was serving that penance for. To all outward appearances, Boyd was truly a reformed man.

But the reformed bank robber still had at least one skeleton kicking around in his closet.

Some stories about Edwin Alonzo Boyd suggest that he turned religious, reading the Bible regularly and offering to help anyone in need while he served his time in the Kingston Pen. Perhaps his conversion was heartfelt. Certainly his friends would have believed so. But in the months leading up to his death in 2002, it appeared that Boyd was struggling to make some kind of restitution, trying to right some past wrong.

In a sense, he was challenged to relive his 80-plus years when noted author Brian Vallee approached him about a book he was writing about Boyd and his infamous gang. During several interviews, the ex-con alluded to a "bad mistake" he'd made in the years leading up to the bank heists. He said he "did a lot of walking in those days" and had decided he needed "to practise" his skills if he ever wanted to make it as a career criminal.

"You know, like when I went in to rob the banks, I was practising—going through a routine until I had it down pat, and then I went ahead and did it," Boyd told Vallee.

Ed Gadzala, owner of Toronto's now defunct Hillcrest Motel, didn't know it at the time, but when he learned how Boyd would practise before robbing a bank, incidents from the past started to make sense.

"They were staying here while they were doing jobs," Gadzala told *Toronto Star* reporter Bill Taylor in 2006 when the paper wrote a story about the famous landmark and its noted guests. "They took three or four rooms, and we could never figure out what all the noise was. They were doing calisthenics, keeping in shape for jumping over bank counters. My mother asked Boyd once, 'What kind of business are you in?' He said, 'The banking business.'"

But it was a different kind of practising Boyd was cryptically referring to when he spoke with Vallee. Boyd wasn't known to display any remorse over his days of pulling bank heists with his gang of thieves, but it was clear that something in his past was weighing heavily on his conscience.

"Some of the things I did were way out over the edge," Boyd said, reluctant to acknowledge exactly what he had done. "…this other thing, I'd have to reveal how I practised that, and that was…that was something that I couldn't possibly talk about…because it would put me right back in prison again."

Slowly, over a series of repeated interviews, Vallee eroded Boyd's resolve. Although he was somewhat obscure about the actual details, Boyd eventually talked about a "walk" he'd taken on the night of September 11, 1947. He talked about a couple of strangers he'd happened upon and how they were "mouthing off what they were going to do." Perhaps they'd seen the Luger and noticed that Boyd seemed to be acting suspiciously, but they weren't savvy enough to keep their comments to themselves.

Boyd finally admitted that he thought the pair was going to turn him in to the police, though he didn't elaborate on what he might have done at that point to instigate such an action. "As far as I was concerned, they knew about me, so that was it," Boyd said. "I knew I would have to get rid of them, so I did.

Back in those days, it didn't bother me. I'd just got out of the army a short time."

Clearly, if Boyd indeed was confessing to the double murder of Iris Scott and George Vigus Sr., it bothered the octogenarian a lot more in 2002 than it had those many years ago. And although he never mentioned their names directly, he did point to the date and the area and confessed that he'd stuffed their bodies into the trunk of their car. A record search of unsolved murders matching that MO in that part of Toronto yielded a single case—that of Scott and Vigus. Boyd didn't need to say their names.

At one point in his career, Boyd had robbed two banks in 10 days. Although he pleaded guilty to eight bank heists, he later told reporters he thought the actual number was closer to 30. Like an actor in an action film, Boyd enjoyed the intrigue his image still provoked.

Perhaps it was his dashing good looks that paved the way for one of Canada's most notorious gangsters to bridge the gap between disgust for his behaviour and his status as a legendary folk hero. Or perhaps Boyd's apparent rehabilitation reinforced the belief that reformation was possible, even in the most dangerous of criminals. Whatever the case, whether they admitted it or not, most Canadians found something likeable in the man. In general, people wished him well.

And despite everything, despite his decades of "penance" and his apparent reform, one incident will forever overshadow Boyd's earlier image as the gentleman bandit, and that was his final interview and the disclosure of the most heinous and senseless crime of his career.

Boyd was no longer just a sweet-hearted man with a smattering of bad blood in his veins. He was also a cold-blooded killer.

Gone Fishing
Tyson Conn

~

I've acquired my 47-year-sentence through common stupidity, a penchant for robbing banks and a very bad habit of either escaping or attempting to get away.

–Tyson Conn in a letter to Brian Vallee,
author of the book *Edwin Alonzo Boyd*

He could feel the adrenalin coursing through his body, pushing his heart into overdrive. Despite the tension a situation like this was bound to incite, the hidden convict restrained any impulse to move, breathing in low, shallow breaths, thereby avoiding detection. He was confident that if he remained calm and stayed in his hiding spot in the corner of the now-empty workroom, he wouldn't be noticed; he had a good feel for the guards on duty that night and knew their routines, their strengths and weaknesses, at least as far as their work habits went. Of course, you never knew when a newbie keener would be on duty or if one of the other guards was feeling in a particularly vigilant mood that night. But 32-year-old convicted bank robber Tyson Conn hadn't landed himself behind the walls of Ontario's Kingston Penitentiary, one of the world's oldest maximum-security prisons still in operation, by playing it safe.

Everything about his plan was risky, but if he escaped, Conn figured the dummy in his bed would provoke the most conversation when people discovered what he had done. He had rolled up a few bits of material, rearranged his pillows and made up his bed to look as though he was sleeping. It was the oldest trick in the book.

Timing, of course, was always the key, and Conn's timing was impeccable. The ruse had to be prepared before his shift in the industrial shop. An observant guard might notice that the inmate's bed looked a little suspicious. If that happened, the inmate's quest for freedom would be shut down before it really began. And then there were the ongoing bed checks throughout the night. Between 4:30 PM on May 6, 1999, and 7:00 AM the next morning, guards peered into Conn's cell at least five times. Suspicion could have risen at any of those bed checks, especially if the guards noticed that the sleeping man hadn't altered his position from one bed check to the next.

Whichever way the dice rolled, Conn had tried to plan for every contingency. It took him quite some time and a lot of ingenuity to avoid detection, but he wove a rope using scraps of materials from the shop area where convicts repaired mailbags and made furniture. Conn was confident that the 12-metre-long rope was sufficient to do the job. The grappling hook he'd crafted from a crowbar was certainly capable of holding his body weight.

When everything quieted down, he planned to cut through the wire window coverings and crawl outside—the shop windows weren't barred, so he didn't have to worry about carving through thick slabs of steel or heavy iron. Once he made it outside, all he had to do was wait until the midnight shift clocked in; Conn knew the southeast tower wasn't manned after midnight. When the tower was empty, all he had left to do was to dodge the video cameras and motion detectors and hurl his body over the wall. If he was quick enough, no one would notice him scale the wall near that tower. Conn banked on being quick enough.

Of course, even the best-laid plans sometimes fail. Conn had no idea if his scheme would pan out as he'd hoped, or if all his hard work would come tumbling down upon him like a house of cards. But at this point in his life, it didn't matter. He had to give it a try. He'd been in jail long enough—longer than some convicts who'd served time for murder. He'd never murdered anybody, and to Conn's way of thinking, he'd more than paid his debt to society.

It was time to leave or go down in a hail of bullets in one last, desperate quest for freedom.

On January 18, 1967, a frightened 16-year-old gave birth to a baby boy she named Earnest Bruce Hayes. With nothing but positive intentions, the young mother had hoped that she and her 27-year-old boyfriend could provide a good home for their baby in Toronto. But as they say, the road to hell is paved with good intentions. Earnest's father soon tired of domesticity, and his mother relinquished her son to the care of his grandparents. By the time the lad was three years old, he had become a ward of the Crown.

Earnest apparently didn't want for a family for long, though. During a psychological assessment of the boy, a Belleville, Ontario-based psychiatrist named Dr. Bert Conn was taken with the clever and spirited child and decided to adopt Earnest and raise him alongside his own three children.

Some might have thought that the youngster, whose name was eventually changed to Tyson William Conn, had caught a lucky break. But things are rarely what they seem. Although the senior Conn and his wife were both professionals—Loris was a psychiatric nurse—and could certainly afford to provide for the material needs of another child, their marriage was under great strain. Loris suffered from depression and was reputedly struggling with alcohol abuse. She resented having to care for another child, and young Tyson became the target at which the frustrated mother could cast all her anger and frustrations. Although there was food on the table and a roof over his head, Tyson never really felt loved and accepted by the couple that adopted him or by his new siblings.

In their book *Who Killed Ty Conn?*, authors Linden MacIntyre and Theresa Burke reflect on Conn's early years and point to the deficits of a rocky childhood as contributing factors in the man he eventually became: "Ty Conn's life lacked the benefit of the most essential and natural and elusive condition of human existence: belonging," they assert. "Ty Conn never belonged, and so his life was shapeless, like something accidentally spilled, flowing into the emptiness around him, a blot on the social fabric."

The theory certainly bore some merit. Being displaced from the only family he'd ever known at such a young and impressionable age left Ty struggling with feelings of abandonment. Those feelings often produce attachment disorders, and when children don't connect to the people they live with, it's human nature that they look elsewhere to fill the void in their life. If Ty had been placed with a family who poured all their love and energies into boosting the young boy's self-image, it's likely his struggles with being abandoned could have been overcome. Clearly, that wasn't what happened. Ty never felt connected to the Conn family, and it was this lack of belonging, and the often unfair manner he was treated in during his formative years that MacIntyre and Burke suggest helped form Ty's personality.

Even as a youngster, Conn demonstrated a propensity toward stealing and then bolting. MacIntyre and Burke described how a quest for food landed six-year-old Tyson in his parents' bad books. He tried to avoid the punishment he sensed was coming by running away. It was the first time he took off. In his mind, it was better to freeze while hiding inside a barn in the middle of winter than to face the Conns' wrath.

After eight years of battling it out with their adopted son and his several forays into foster care and group homes, the Conns decided to relinquish the boy. Tyson was back in the system and more desperate than ever to take care of himself the only way he knew how—by taking whatever he needed and avoiding detection.

You can only skirt the authorities for so long, however. In 1984, by the time Conn was 17, he'd held up a corner store at gunpoint. The storeowner slashed at the boy with a knife, and although most would argue that a gun trumps a knife every time, the young thief fled the scene empty-handed. In retrospect, it makes perfect sense that Conn hadn't pushed the issue. By his own admission years later, he never had any intention of hurting anyone in the commission of his exploits. Still, his use of a gun succeeded in painting him as a bandit who was "armed and dangerous" in the minds of the public and the law alike.

Not about to let a little thing like a bungled store robbery discourage him, Conn went on to Plan B—robbing banks. Even though he was just a teen, he knew that bank employees were taught to hand over the cash rather than argue with a robber and face potential injury or death. Conn had no doubt he'd profit from this kind of heist. He just needed to make sure he thoroughly planned every aspect of his getaway and moved quickly.

It takes a certain kind of intelligence to successfully pull off an armed robbery before authorities pin you down. Conn was both intelligent and successful. He robbed several banks in Ottawa and Toronto and lived to spend the spoils of his labour before moving on to banks in rural locations. And he preferred to target smaller communities like Napanee. "I kind of like robbing banks in rural areas where the nearest OPP [Ontario Provincial Police] had to travel at least 15 or 20 miles to respond to a robbery," Conn once said in a letter to Brian Vallee, author of the book *Edwin Alonzo Boyd*. But even with the gap between the time police arrived on scene and when they began tracking Conn down, the law did eventually catch up with him. Although he was still a minor at the time of his initial offences and capture, Conn had to do hard time at a federal penitentiary.

Conn's first taste of freedom came in March 1987 after he was arrested and found guilty of robbery in 1984. At that point, the 20-year-old had served a sufficient amount of his sentence that he was granted release on "mandatory supervision." Almost as soon as he stepped outside the prison walls, Conn and two other culprits pointed a sawed-off shotgun in the face of a teller at a west-end bank in Ottawa. Conn and his conspirators were arrested later that same day.

If Conn had any intention of walking the straight-and-narrow path of a law-abiding citizen, it certainly wasn't happening.

That Conn found it difficult to bide his time behind bars is clear when reviewing his repeated rebellion during the periods of incarceration he endured in his short life. Yet it's strange to note that in 1989, Conn pulled his first Houdini-like escape by extricating himself from a prison escort. It was the same year he was eligible for day parole—all he had to do was hold on a short while longer and he would be allowed to spend time in the outside world. When he ditched his escort, it was almost as if the convicted robber wanted to be recaptured—perhaps he wanted to return to life behind bars in the only environment where he quite likely ever felt he belonged. Still, if there was any cognitive dissonance over his actions, it didn't prevent Conn from becoming one of Ontario's most wanted men for almost 10 weeks. When police finally captured the fugitive after 68 days on the run, it meant more than just a return to jail. His escape, coupled with the jobs he'd pulled during his self-administered freedom, landed him additional sentences.

At 10:45 PM on November 5, 1991, Conn escaped custody once again. This time he'd been incarcerated in the Collin's Bay Institution, a medium-security federal penitentiary also located in Kingston. It was at Collin's Bay where Conn first scaled a six-metre-high, fortress-like wall separating him from his freedom. Prison spokesman Ron Fairley told reporters that Conn had disappeared by the time guards responded to the alarm triggered by his escape. Fairley said the six-metre-long ladder Conn had used "was stuff he kind of just cabbaged together—metal and wood and stuff…he was able to get over the wall extremely quickly."

Conn also built the homemade hacksaw he used to cut through the bars in a bathroom window. He'd collected maps and meticulously planned his escape route. One news article explained how a search of the convict's cell and possessions following his escape produced "articles on winter outdoor survival, shelter building, and knife and tomahawk throwing." Conn had left nothing to chance. He'd even left a parting message to the prison guards on his calendar, scrawling the words "Gone Fishing" across the date of that prison break.

Conn eluded the authorities for a month following the Collin's Bay escape. During that time, he robbed one Ottawa bank, and then another. His third Ottawa-area heist was the Guarantee Trust. The police were on the scene a lot quicker that time. Conn fled on foot, breaking into an apartment building and attempting to jump from one balcony to another before finding himself in an all-out standoff with the authorities. He was tried and found guilty of all three robberies, earning himself the title of Canada's "modern-day Houdini." He also had several additional sentences tacked on to the ones he was already serving. Barely into his 20s, Tyson Conn was staring at a 47-year sentence. If he was lucky, he might get out by 2017. If he remained behind bars for the entire 47 years, it would be 2032 before he was a free man.

For a man who couldn't stand being confined, even though prison was almost the only "home" he'd ever known, the years ahead loomed heavier than a death sentence.

At the Kingston Penitentiary, Ty Conn was uniformly viewed as one of the good guys by his fellow inmates. A report issued by the *Kingston Whig-Standard* profiled Conn shortly after his historic 1999 escape from the prison. Thirty-three-year-old William Stoddart told reporter Rob Tripp that he and other inmates who knew Conn were happy to see him escape from the miserable confines of the Kingston Pen. "People just like him and wish him well," Stoddart said.

Although Conn's May 6, 1999, escape was the first for the maximum federal prison in four decades, there had been other successful escapes during the almost two centuries of the prison's history. One source suggests that convicts had tried to scale its walls at least 26 times. But with each attempted escape, prison administration resolved problems in security and made it more difficult for the next potential escapee to break free. At the same time, Stoddart said security wasn't that great at the Kingston Pen, and he wasn't surprised that Conn had made it out. "I've always wondered why people stayed here when they didn't have to," he said. As a last, curious detail, Conn hearkened back to his 1991 escape from Collin's Bay and again wrote a note to the guards on his calendar. This one simply read: "Fishing trip '99."

Prison staff certainly didn't share Stoddart's opinion about the ease with which someone could break out of the Kingston Pen. "I don't see how [Conn] could have escaped without being detected," Assistant Warden John Oddie told the *National Post*. While police were busy organizing a manhunt for the fugitive, Kingston guards were worried about the ramifications on their ranks because of Conn's escape. Corrections Canada would eventually launch a full investigation into the matter.

One thing that officials and inmates did agree upon was the assessment of Conn as a nice guy. "He appeared to keep to himself. There was no indication of violence toward guards or other inmates," Oddie told reporters.

Conn was also smart and resourceful. He'd finished his high school education and studied sociology and psychology while in prison. He also scrounged together the materials he needed for a successful escape in an institution where everything is under strict control. "Chains, hooks and ropes are kept continually locked up by staff," Oddie said. "He must have been a real scrounger." Conn's reputation as a modern-day Houdini once again hit the headlines of big city dailies as they reported his third, and most daring, escape yet.

His resourcefulness continued once he was out in the general population. At about 2:30 PM on Tuesday, May 18, 1999, Conn pulled up to the CIBC in Colborne brandishing a sawed-off shotgun and demanding money. After receiving an undisclosed amount of cash, Conn jumped into the 1977 Buick Le Sabre he'd allegedly pilfered sometime on Sunday night and took off. Even with the use of a Trenton-based search-and-rescue helicopter that happened to be flying in the area at the time, police lost the escaped convict's trail.

But Conn's last skirmish with the law was rapidly coming to an end.

※

There is a lot of truth to the old adage that there is no honour among thieves. Conn might have thought he'd found a momentary reprieve in the Toronto home of a one-time friend and ex-convict, Paul Texiera, but he was sadly mistaken. The party rocking his friend's pad made him nervous. There were so many people. People he didn't know were learning that Ontario's most wanted man was holed up there, and it created a bigger buzz than all the alcohol on site.

Conn was not addicted to drugs or alcohol, and he'd never shown himself to be an angry man prone to uncontrolled outbursts. But that night in Texiera's home, hiding from the authorities and overwhelmed by his situation, he indulged in heroin. It left him sick and paralyzed, unable to wade his way through the tidal wave of emotions he was feeling. Conn wrote a letter to Burke just a couple of months before his escape, and its contents revealed a man who'd lost hope. "It seems I'm doomed to pay for past mistakes forever with these people, and they can't be convinced that I just want to get out of jail legally," he wrote. "I'm going to put some thought into changing tactics."

As far as Conn could see, he had no other choice than to plan that last and final escape or die trying.

Gone Fishing
Tyson Conn

Conn spent the majority of the next day on the couch. At about 9:00 PM, the sirens wailing in the distance approached Texiera's house, waking Conn in the process. Police had the house surrounded. Once again, Conn found himself alone. Had his one-time friend tipped off the authorities?

The police began calling his name and ordered him to surrender. Instead of turning himself over to the authorities, Conn pointed his shotgun into his chest and threatened to pull the trigger if police didn't keep their distance.

The desperate man did agree, however, to speak on the telephone with either Linden MacIntyre or Theresa Burke; Conn had first met the reporters five years earlier when they were preparing a story for the *Fifth Estate*. It was Burke who, in the end, tried to convince the tired, distraught man to surrender.

"I've thought about it," Conn said. "I was willing to pay for my crimes.... But I've paid with 18 years, and I can't go back there."

At one point during their conversation, Conn told Burke that he had to move because the reception on his cell phone was spotty. Conn started talking again, having found a new place in the house to sit. Burke said the man spoke two words—although she could never remember what those words were, she knew there were two. And then she heard "a pop and the phone crashing to the floor."

Tyson Cobb's traumatic journey was finally over, but not in the way anyone had expected. The 32-year-old was dead from what Burke believed was an accidentally self-inflicted gunshot wound.

Just days before his last robbery, Conn had visited his birth mother. The two had developed what some described as a "warm relationship" over the years. It was somewhat comforting to think that the young man who felt so alone had reconnected in a meaningful way with the woman who had brought him into the world.

Still, as far as Burke was concerned, Conn should have been someone who could have emerged from the system a better man than when he entered. "He had no drug or alcohol problems. He wasn't emotionally out of control," Burke told reporter David Stonehouse. "He wasn't angry. So if he is not rehabilitatable, maybe we should be looking at the system and saying that something should be done differently—because he was salvageable."

In the end, the man with the ongoing quest for freedom had gone fishing for the last time.

Miramichi Menace
Allan Legere

A police video at Allan Legere's murder trial yesterday showed Smith's crumpled body lying face down in front of the locked vault, a large gash across one hand. The Roman Catholic priest's face had been pulverized and the back pockets of his pants were torn off...

–from "Lock was no help, Trial told of priest's slaying,"
Canadian Press article, September 20, 1991

The city of Miramichi bills itself as a "great place to live, work and play!" And for the most part, it's exactly that. With a population of just over 18,000, Miramichi is New Brunswick's largest city and is located at the mouth of the Miramichi River. But before the city was even formed by the amalgamation of the communities of Newcastle and Chatham in 1995, the area was famous. Sadly, it wasn't the quaint architecture, the East Coast charm or the countless opportunities for adventure that propelled the city into the public spotlight. Instead, it was the name of one man and his reputation as the "Monster of Miramichi."

It's the oldest ruse in the book, and that's probably why it worked. No one would have expected someone to try something so bold and brassy. On Wednesday, May 3, 1989, 41-year-old Allan Legere was complaining of an ear infection. Prison staff did what they could to ease his pain, but it looked like the prisoner needed more medical intervention than they could provide. He would have to be transported from the maximum-security prison at Renous, where he was being incarcerated, to a hospital in Moncton. The transfer certainly wasn't anything out of the ordinary. Prisoners need special medical attention all the time, so no one thought twice about it. It wasn't as if Legere was reclining on a cot, no chains attached and free to move about as he pleased. No, there was plenty of iron restraining the man's hands and feet.

No one expected that during his incarceration, Legere had gathered together the items he needed to create a makeshift key—a key that he used to unlock his restraints when the two guards escorting the convict allowed him a bathroom break. No one expected that Legere had also smuggled in some kind of crude but effective weapon. And no one thought it possible that he could overcome two guards. Yet that is exactly what Legere did.

The prisoner's successful escape from custody made the authorities look bad, but that certainly wasn't the most disturbing part of the situation. The convict was up to some of his old tricks. Considering that he'd spent the previous seven years serving a life sentence for the brutal murder of a 66-year-old shopkeeper, news that he was at large and quite possibly on the hunt again had residents of the area double-checking the locks on their doors.

For days following Legere's escape, police scoured a 20-square-kilometre wooded area in west Moncton where they believed the con was hiding out. The day after Legere's escape, police learned of an overnight break-in at a construction shack. They believed Legere was responsible for that break in because it seemed that the culprit responsible was just interested in using the cot and was not looking to steal anything.

For a while, the authorities were hot on the convict's heels. Having tracked Legere in 1982, police were well versed in his evasion techniques: his habit of crisscrossing his tracks, fording streams, changing shoes, doubling back on his trail—the fugitive knew every trick in the book. But their familiarity with his methods, as well as help from tracking dogs and a surveillance helicopter, should have given the authorities the upper hand. At one point, after an intense, 14-hour chase, the authorities thought they were closing in and Legere's capture was imminent, but the chase ended with the convict still on the loose.

It took officials almost seven months before they managed to cuff the man and put him back behind bars where he belonged.

Sadly, Legere would leave a trail of victims in his wake.

Not long after his escape, Legere committed his first heinous murder—a brutal attack on a pair of elderly women on May 28. Nina Flam only remembers bits and pieces of the night she was raped and beaten, and her 75-year-old sister-in-law, Annie, was murdered in the women's Chatham, New Brunswick, home. That she was alive to remember anything was a miracle. For more than three hours, 63-year-old Nina wrestled with her attacker as he sexually assaulted, beat and burned her.

"He said he would set fire to the house, and when they found my body, they would think it was an accident," Nina told the court during Legere's trial. Not only did Nina survive the rape and beating, but she also recovered from third-degree burns to more than 40 percent of her body. Annie was raped and beaten to death before Leger set the fire that consumed most of her body.

Legere was considered a suspect in the attack on Nina and Annie, but the fugitive was as elusive as ever. Police still didn't have any idea where he might be hiding out, and the fire had destroyed a good portion of the evidence at the scene. At the same time, the authorities had to keep an open mind and consider every possibility if they were to find the monster responsible for this loathsome crime.

Five months later, on October 13, a similar attack on two sisters living in Newcastle, New Brunswick, reminded area residents that a demon was still on the loose. The feeling that no one was safe in their own homes was reinforced after news of a double-murder emerged in the media. It looked like the suspect in this case broke through back door of the home where 41-year-old Linda Daughney lived with her sister, Donna, aged 43. Once he'd gained entry, there was no stopping the man. The sisters' bodies were discovered shortly after firefighters arrived at their burning home. The blaze was contained before the crime scene was completely obliterated, and what investigators found was beyond barbaric. A pair of blood-soaked jeans was discovered on a staircase. And there was so much blood smeared throughout the house that it seemed as if the perpetrator had deliberately spread it around after he'd murdered the women.

Roy Geike, a firefighter at the scene that day, later testified that the sisters' bodies were so badly mutilated that the only way anyone could identify the women was because one sister was bigger than the other. "I was looking to see who it was because I knew Linda and Donna very well…I couldn't tell. The face was bruised and swollen and both eyes were quite puffy. Blood covered the eyes."

By now it was clear to everyone that until the individual responsible for these vicious crimes was apprehended, the carnage would continue. But the villain's choice of his next victim surprised everyone.

On Thursday, November 16, 1989, Father James Smith was in his rectory near Chatham Head, thinking about saying his evening offices and preparing for bed, when he heard a loud crash. The noise startled him, and a feeling of doom fell over the

Nativity of the Blessed Virgin Mary church's 69-year-old priest. Over the last several months, a crime spree consisting of murder, robbery, arson and even rape had overwhelmed the Miramichi area, and residents were living in terror. No one was safe. People were talking about sleeping with their guns—locks weren't sufficient to protect anyone from the culprit or culprits responsible. Smith was likely wondering if he was about to come face to face with a demon.

He would not live to tell the tale. The next day, the priest's bloodied, lifeless body was found in a crumpled heap on his office floor. The door of the large, walk-in vault located in the room was still securely fastened, but someone had tried desperately to break it open. An axe, chisel, drill and ice pick were found beside the body. Whoever broke into the rectory had crushed the deadbolt on the front door with an axe and followed through by kicking the door in with his boots. It was clear that the person responsible for turning Smith's face into hamburger was intent on clearing out any money or valuables the vault might have contained. The perpetrator didn't gain a cent in the robbery attempt, but the destruction left behind turned the usually peaceful setting into a grisly crime scene.

News of Father Smith's murder further terrorized an already frightened community. The carnage of the last few months had to stop. Just two days earlier, residents had every reason to expect a reprieve, especially those who didn't buy the theory that escaped convict Allan Legere was responsible for some of the more gruesome crimes that had occurred during the last several months.

On November 15, Allard Joseph Vienneau had appeared in court after being arrested for a string of crimes that included several assaults and break-and-enters. But even with Vienneau's arrest, police were cautioning residents not to get too complacent. Vienneau wasn't a suspect in the previous month's sexual assault and murder of two sisters who lived together in Newcastle. Nor was the 30-year-old charged with the beating of two elderly sisters in Chatham several months earlier. Although they were trying to maintain an open-minded approach and didn't want to have "tunnel vision" during their investigations, police still believed the man responsible for those crimes was Legere. They were fingering Legere with Smith's murder as well, and the report of a "lone, long-haired man" driving the priest's stolen Oldsmobile seemed to reinforce that theory.

If people were frightened before, it was nothing compared to how they felt after Smith's murder. Who would stoop so low as to kill a man of God? For investigators who attended the crime scene and collected the good priest's body, it was clear that only a monster could have done such a thing.

Officials doubled their already tireless efforts in hunting down their main suspect. Legere was being compared to Charles Manson, and police warned the public that the convict, who'd already been found guilty of the charge of murder, was a "charismatic killer with persuasive powers." Eight days after Father Smith's murder, following a dramatic standoff and an overnight hostage-taking incident, police succeeded in capturing their prey.

RCMP Corporal Terry Barter was able to stop Legere with a kick to the head when the convict was cornered near Nelson, New Brunswick. Barter explained how Legere was indignant at officer's actions and accused him of being "just as bad as me. You're just an animal." Barter held his ground, keeping Legere facedown on a highway near Chatham Head while the suspect was handcuffed. Barter described Legere as a small, shrivelled man who almost looked timid. "He was scared.... He said, 'I never hurt any of your guys. I didn't hurt the policewoman. I didn't hurt the dog.'"

Legere was charged with Smith's murder as well as with the sexual assault and murder of Annie Flam, the assault of Nina Flam and the sex slayings of Donna Daughney and her sister, Linda. He was found guilty of all four murders, and his trial made Canadian criminal history as being the "first criminal case in the country decided by DNA evidence alone."

Legere is still known as the Monster of Miramichi, but that monster is confined in a Québec-based, super-max facility—a Security Housing Unit nicknamed the "SHU." Despite his repeated requests to be transferred to a maximum-security prison in New Brunswick, the province's public safety minister, John Foran, assured his worried constituents as recently as 2008 that Legere would remain incarcerated in the

SHU. "[Federal public safety minister Stockwell Day] assured me that there's no way Mr. Legere would be moved back to New Brunswick, there's no way that his status in prison is going to be downgraded, and he's not being transferred," Foran told Canadian Press reporters.

For now, the residents of the Miramichi region can sleep. But memories of the deadly monster who once lived in their midst isn't something that can be easily put to rest.

At All Costs
James Charles Kopp

~

*I was innocent of murder then. I am innocent of murder
now. I have separated murderers from their weapons
of mass destruction.*

–James Charles Kopp

The man who drove the black Chevrolet Cavalier, licence plate number BPE 216, took his time cruising through the Roxbury Park neighbourhood of Amherst, New York, where Dr. Barnett Slepian made his residence. There was no reason for anyone to be overly concerned about the man's presence. But the car had shown up fairly often in the preceding days and weeks and didn't appear to belong to anyone in the neighbourhood, so it must have made at least a couple of people uneasy, especially since witnesses later came forward to say they remembered the vehicle.

When images of the driver were made public, several more witnesses also recognized the man as the same person who had jogged through the neighbourhood on the morning of October 23, 1998, but nobody knew him personally. Could this stranger have had anything to do with what happened around 10:00 PM that same night, when the evening silence was shattered by the sound of a single rifle shot that killed Dr. Slepian just two days after his 52nd birthday?

Police didn't come right out and call the man they initially labelled as John Doe a suspect in the sniper-style murder of the well-known and much-loved Dr. Barnett Slepian. But in November 1998, authorities in both the United States and Canada publicly announced that they were looking for a man they had by then identified as James Charles Kopp. They wanted to interview him about the recent tragedy, though they didn't elaborate on the reasons for their interest. Police did state that once the man was located, he would be arrested on a federal material witness warrant.

Aside from perhaps a brief mention, Canadian news agencies normally don't follow a murder case that occurs south of the border too closely. But the fact that Canadian authorities were also looking for the man and were somewhat less than forthcoming about the reasons behind that preoccupation more than piqued the curiosity of reporters in newsrooms across the country.

Of course, holding back information from a reporter is more apt to raise curiosity than quell it, and it wasn't long before it was discovered that Dr. Slepian was the most recent in what appeared to be a string of assaults on physicians. On November 5, a story released by Sun Media drew attention to the wounding of four other doctors, three of them in Canada and another in upstate New York. In each case, a sniper hiding somewhere around the doctors' homes had pulled the trigger of a rifle, unleashing a potentially lethal bullet in the direction of its intended target. All of the attacks occurred around November 11—a day that some anti-abortion extremists had adopted as a "day of protest," and a connection between the attacks and the annual pro-life event was noted. All four victims were obstetrician-gynecologists who performed abortions, just like Dr. Slepian. "All of the shootings are linked," Winnipeg Police Inspector Keith McCaskill told reporters from Hamilton's *Spectator*. "Anything this guy [Kopp] can provide us with, we are interested in."

The possible Canadian connection between the murders was becoming clearer. But how did the man they were looking for figure into the equation? Journalists started digging into Kopp's background and came up with some interesting information that might explain what it was about his past that caught the interest of authorities.

James Charles Kopp was born in Pasadena, California, on August 2, 1954. His father was an ex-Marine who made his living as a lawyer, and his mother was a nurse. It appeared that Kopp had many of the advantages of youth and that his parents were able to meet his needs and, quite likely, most of his wants.

But Kopp later explained how things started to change for him in 1980 after he saw an aborted fetus in Stanford Hospital in Palo Alto, California. The incident weighed so heavily on the sensitive young man that he credited it with propelling him into the pro-life movement.

But Kopp's extreme reaction to what he'd seen drove him beyond his initial disgust into the public spotlight and into the bad books of several police departments across the United States. In November 1986, Kopp forcibly blocked the entrance to an abortion clinic in Pensacola, Florida. He refused to move, even for the police, and he further resisted arrest, making him an increasingly unpopular fellow with law enforcement personnel in that city.

In July 1988, Kopp experienced a run-in with the law in Atlanta, Georgia, when he was arrested for taking part in an anti-abortion demonstration at the Democratic National Convention being held in that city. It was at this event where Kopp earned the moniker "Atomic Dog."

In 1991, Kopp and an unnamed accomplice caused a headache for Long Island police when they locked their feet together in front of a Levittown clinic. Authorities had to dismantle the steel device connecting the two protestors before escorting them to the nearest police detachment.

On another occasion, Kopp was one of several hundred protesters arrested in Burlington, Vermont, at the pro-life demonstration dubbed Operation Rescue, and he was also arrested in

New York during a similar protest demonstration at an abortion clinic in that city.

Regardless of what the police were willing to share about the details surrounding their interest in Kopp, the media was certainly painting a fairly damning picture of the man who was beginning to look less the part of a knight in shining armour saving unborn babies from an early grave and more and more like a potential murder suspect.

It was the evening of November 10, 1995. Winter was just around the corner, and that night, it was cold and raining in Ancaster, Ontario, a community just east of Hamilton. The damp weather sent a chill through anyone who was unlucky enough to be outside.

Sixty-two-year-old Dr. Hugh Short was at home in his second-floor den, likely preparing to make his way to bed, when he heard a shot and felt a bullet sear through his flesh and shatter his elbow. But before he could take cover, another shot was fired. Short collapsed to the ground. Were it not for his wife, Katherine, who rushed to his side and tied a tourniquet around his wound, the doctor would have bled to death before help arrived. Thanks to his spouse's quick action, Dr. Short survived. The attack did not end his life, but it did end his career.

The seemingly random act of violence that changed the course of Dr. Short's life just doesn't happen in our country, especially in upscale neighbourhoods like the one where he lived. It seemed so senseless, so unbelievable. Who would have wanted to hurt a man who'd taken an oath and dedicated his life to helping people? What could the good doctor have possibly done to push someone to commit such a heinous act of aggression? There had to be some kind of personal connection between the victim and his attacker.

It is unclear when the connection between the attacks on the two doctors was made, but at some point, the authorities recalled the case of Dr. Garson Romalis. On November 8, 1994, a sniper had positioned himself outside Romalis' Vancouver home and, armed with a high-powered rifle, shot him. Romalis sustained a bullet wound to the thigh in that incident, but no one was ever arrested for the shooting. Dr. Short's attack seemed to echo that of his colleague on the other side of the country. And it was soon apparent there was another similarity between the two men—they both performed abortions.

The dots were being connected, even that early on in the investigation, but it wasn't until January 24, 2000, that the Ontario Provincial Police (OPP) issued a warrant for Kopp's arrest. By then, Kopp was a suspect in the murder of Dr. Slepian. He was also suspected of being involved in the attempted shooting of Dr. David Gandell; on October 28, 1997, a sniper took aim at the doctor from Rochester, New York, but Gandell was not injured in the incident. Two weeks later, as if frustrated by the failed attempt, the same attacker was believed to have struck again on November 11 when Dr. Jack Fainman became the victim of a sniper's bullet. The Winnipeg doctor was shot in the shoulder but survived his ordeal. All the doctors targeted by the random sniper routinely performed abortions.

Unlike the previous announcement that police on both sides of the border were looking for Kopp and wanted to interview him about these attacks, there was now no doubt what their intention was. On January 24, 2000, a Canada-wide warrant for Kopp was issued for the attempted murder of Dr. Hugh Short in 1995. Although police didn't feel they had enough evidence to press charges in the attacks on Dr. Fainman or Dr. Romalis, they wanted to talk to Kopp about those shootings as well.

By the time Canadian authorities informed the public that they were looking for Kopp, he was already a wanted man in the U.S. Aside from the circumstantial evidence provided by witnesses who said they'd seen the man in Dr. Slepian's neighbourhood in 1998, on the day the doctor was murdered, investigators in the U.S. had collected what they considered to be solid proof of Kopp's guilt. Back in December 1998, investigators had recovered Kopp's car, which had been abandoned at New Jersey's Newark International Airport. They also recovered a package of bullets, as well as law enforcement's much-coveted DNA evidence—a strand of hair found near Slepian's home was linked to Kopp. And on April 8, 1999, police discovered Kopp's SKS rifle, which had been buried near the crime scene. For the authorities, it was now clearer than ever that Kopp was responsible for Dr. Slepian's death, and they had the proof to back their claims. On October 23, 1999, Kopp was indicted for second-degree murder. Shortly thereafter, his name was added to the FBI's Top 10 Most Wanted list.

It took a bit longer for Canadian officials to move on an arrest warrant because the evidence they had accumulated against Kopp was mostly circumstantial. Although officials in Winnipeg and Vancouver reported that Kopp's car was seen crossing the border not long after the attacks in those cities, they didn't have the physical evidence they needed to nail their case. It was the situation in Ancaster that turned the tables for Canadian investigators. A hat found near the attack on Dr. Short contained hair, and when lab technologists ran the DNA, they found a match to Kopp.

The case against the wanted man was growing by the moment. The problem was that no one had come forward to say they'd seen or heard from Kopp since he disappeared 11 days after Dr. Slepian's death. He hadn't been seen at the rundown farmhouse he shared with a roommate on the outskirts of Swanton, Vermont. "It's like he can disappear—it's very strange," Denise Crawford, manager of a gas station in Swanton, told Sun Media reporter Jon Wells.

Police officials warned the public to be on the lookout for a white male of medium build, 5-foot-10 and weighing somewhere between 150 and 175 pounds. They explained that Kopp had a ruddy complexion, reddish-brown hair, blue-grey eyes and a scar near the thumb of his left hand. He wore glasses, walked with a limp and was a practising Catholic. In the past, he'd worked as a caterer, a construction worker and an electrician. It appeared that Kopp was willing to take any kind of work. He was also described as a dangerous man who might be armed.

The pro-life movement in Canada gained momentum in the late 1960s after Pierre Elliott Trudeau, who was justice minister at the time, introduced an abortion reform bill in 1967. Most people who call themselves pro-life advocates follow the religious belief that life is a gift from God, that all life is sacred and that life begins at conception. That respect for the sanctity of life extends to everyone, including doctors who perform abortions. Peaceful protests and demonstrations are common methods that supporters on both sides of the debate use to publicize their beliefs.

At the same time, there are always radicals who choose to take their philosophy to the extreme. A public tussle between the pro-choice and pro-life segments of society are sometimes more vocal in the U.S. and often more dramatic. Christmas Day 1984 is a case in point. That day, a group of anti-abortionists led by Randall Terry bombed three abortion clinics. They called their act a "birthday gift for Jesus."

Kopp was one of those pro-lifers who couldn't contain the outrage he felt over what he believed was a sinful practice.

The inability to control his anger led him to carry out actions that some would categorize as extreme. His initial interest in the pro-life movement grew into an obsession, and when he started to find peaceful demonstrations ineffective in changing public policy and making abortion illegal, he took the law into his own hands.

Still, it was impossible for the people who knew Kopp to believe he could become aggressive. "Jim no way could have shot an abortionist," Joan Andrews Bell told Laura Bobak of the *Toronto Sun* in April 1999. In Bell's view, it was more likely that investigators planted the evidence against the wanted protestor. "I wouldn't put it past them at all."

According to Bell, an anti-abortion activist who speaks out publicly against the pro-choice movement, Kopp was a pacifist. Although Bell denounced the shooting of a doctor in his or her own home, she voiced considerably different views on the use of violence against doctors entering their clinic or, what she called, an abortion mill. "If they're shot as they're walking into an abortion mill, I will accept whatever the church teaches on that—whether it's justifiable homicide, like a policeman shooting a terrorist," Bell said. "There is a right to use force.... If I condemn that, then I have to condemn every policeman that ever shot a terrorist...if the pro-lifer must be condemned, then the policeman must be condemned."

Some pro-life supporters believed that taking the life of a doctor was in some cases, and in the eyes of God, justifiable.

Shockingly, there appeared to be enough people who backed Kopp's alleged actions that they shielded him from facing prosecution. There were rumours that he had fled to Mexico by January 1999, aided by a female friend who may have driven the fugitive across the border once Kopp realized he needed to take refuge.

There were also stories floating around in Hamilton, Ontario, that Kopp had been identified by *Hamilton Spectator* employees as the man who left five cryptic, anti-abortion threats at the newspaper. So despite border officials not recording his car crossing the Canadian border, it looked as though Kopp somehow made it as far as Hamilton.

Police eventually pieced together Kopp's movements, starting off with pro-life extremists Dennis John Malvasi and Loretta Claire Marra, who allegedly harboured the fugitive in their Brooklyn apartment for a time. The fact that Kopp's car was found at the Newark airport suggested he had travelled to New Jersey before heading elsewhere.

Kopp's disappearing act eventually took him to Ireland, the only European country where abortion is illegal and where Precious Life, a pro-life group with a reputation of being the largest and most radical in the United Kingdom, is based. Kopp knew he'd find kindred spirits in that country, and officials believe he went by the alias Timothy Gottler and lived in a 100-year-old hostel in Dublin before moving on to France. "He had been living in hostels and doing clerical-type work…the Irish police were about 48 hours behind him," FBI Special Agent Joel Mercer told reporters in Buffalo, New York.

Although he was working, Kopp was struggling to make ends meet. On Thursday, March 29, 2001, Kopp was finally apprehended while leaving a post office in Dinan, France—some of Kopp's American supporters had sent him $300 to help him financially. Sources later suggested that wiretaps placed on telephones of radical anti-abortionists in the U.S. had played a part in Kopp's arrest. It was those wiretaps that led investigators to Ireland. Kopp was increasingly aware that after being on the run for more than two years, investigators were closing in on him. The fugitive fled to France on March 12, 2001, but his new start in a new country was short-lived.

Although he was in custody, Kopp was still a long way from being brought to justice as far as Canadian and American officials were concerned. Before the French government was willing to extradite the criminal, they demanded assurance that the pro-lifer wouldn't receive the death penalty for his crimes—capital punishment was abolished in France in 1981. On June 28, two months after his capture, a French court recommended the extradition after being assured that Kopp would receive a fair trial in the United States on the charges of murder and of "violating the federal Freedom of Access to Clinic Entrances Act by using deadly force against a doctor who performs abortions."

Canada would have to wait and see if Kopp would ever face a Canadian court, but authorities here were thrilled at the arrest, taking comfort in the fact that Kopp wouldn't be able to exercise his particular brand of justice in the future.

"We've said all along that he is the key to offences not solved in Canada. His arrest brings new life to the entire investigation," McCaskill told Sun Media reporter Greg Di Cresce. "But the bottom line is that he is brought to justice."

Of course, Kopp appealed the French court's decision to extradite him, but in May 2002, he waived his right to continue his appeal and returned to the U.S. In March 2003, Kopp further waived his right to be tried by jury, still convinced that his actions were noble. "If I see someone attacking a pregnant woman or their children, I'm gonna do something," he told the court. When asked how he could possibly think that shooting the physician with a high-powered rifle wouldn't lead to Dr. Slepian's death, Kopp admitted he couldn't be sure the bullet intended to injure the man wouldn't kill him. "There's never 100-percent certainty.... But I was certain he'd kill 25 children the next day."

The fact that Kopp argued he had no intention of killing Dr. Slepian had no impact on Erie County Judge Michael D'Amico, and on May 9, 2003, D'Amico found Kopp guilty of second-degree murder. During Kopp's sentencing, D'Amico told Kopp, "It's clear the act is premeditated; there is no doubt about it. You made an attempt to avoid responsibility for the act. What may appear righteous to you is immoral to someone else."

Kopp's attorney appealed the decision, but an appellate court upheld it.

Kopp received 25 years to life on the charge of second-degree murder, but his legal battles were far from over. He eventually went to trial for violating federal law protecting access to abortion services. He was convicted on January 25, 2007, and given an additional life sentence.

Kopp remained undaunted by his legal predicament. He told federal judge Richard Arcara that he "may have a plan for me for 25 or 30 years, but Jesus has a plan for me for 20 or 30 billion years. I'll go with door number two."

Kopp's supporters watched teary-eyed as the man clad in an orange jumpsuit was led out of the courtroom.

On May 26, 2009, charges against Kopp in the shooting of Dr. Short were stayed. The case is not closed, however. And Kopp is still considered a "person of interest" in that attempted murder, as well as the other three unsolved shootings.

That Kopp will ever stand trial for those assaults is unlikely at this point. On the rare occasions that Kopp has agreed to speak with the media, he has purposely steered clear of discussing the Canadian shootings, and he has refused to speak with members of the Ontario Provincial Police when they visited the American jail Kopp now calls home. But it's a moot point really, at least as far as Dr. Short is concerned. In May 2009, Short told Jon Wells, a reporter with the *Hamilton Spectator*, that he wasn't concerned about the Canadian authorities' decision to drop the charges against Kopp, and he wasn't worried about them looking for another suspect. Without mentioning Kopp's name, Dr. Short suggested that the person responsible for his attack had already been sentenced.

Although James Charles Kopp might not have been convicted of the Canadian crimes he's suspected of committing in the weeks around Remembrance Day, the sporadic shootings of doctors who perform abortions appear to have ceased since his incarceration.

Childhood Horror
RICHARD STEVE GOLDBERG

~

> *Goldberg gained the trust of* [neighbourhood] *parents and then befriended their children. He entertained the girls by allowing them to play with his pets, watch television and use his computer to play games. Some of these girls also took short trips with him…*
>
> —June 2002 FBI press release

To those who knew him, Richard Steve Goldberg must have seemed innocuous enough. Certainly, it was a bit odd that the single, one-time aerospace engineer had for whatever reason left a good-paying job at Boeing to make an extreme career change and venture into the world of babysitting. Still, personal evolution is part of a healthy life, some would argue. Circumstances lend themselves to new possibilities, and the path that once proved so fulfilling and profitable had perhaps lost its charm.

Whatever the reason, it appears that some time in 2001, Goldberg replaced a demanding and competitive career with more lighthearted work and filled his home and yard with computer games and outside play structures. Once he'd transformed his living space, he tagged a childcare provider entry on to his résumé and opened his doors to the neighbourhood youngsters, advertising his services to working parents in the Long Beach area of California. He must have seemed safe and legitimate to the moms and dads who entrusted their beloved children into his care while they were busy making a living for their families. But as Helen Keller once said, security is mostly a superstition.

In this case, the impression of security was a dangerous superstition, indeed.

In May 2001, Long Beach police received a disturbing complaint. After being picked up at their babysitter's home, two young girls began to regale their parents with stories about their day. That day, however, the stories weren't anything like the tales of recess games or friends or worries about school that typically fleshed out the dinnertime chatter. What these girls told their parents sent shock waves that not only shattered their lives but also reverberated throughout their community and across the state. They said that while playing on Goldberg's computer, they came across naked pictures of their babysitter and two young girls about their age.

If these girls were concerned enough over their discovery to share what they'd found with their parents, their parents were horrified. As soon as they reported their daughters' story to the authorities, police launched an investigation. In June 2001, officers raided the 56-year-old man's home, arrested the suspect and seized his computer.

The contents of Goldberg's computer appeared to support the young girls' story about the photos they found. Even more disturbing was that more than just the two girls had been taken advantage of by their after-school childcare provider. Six children eventually came forward, claiming they had been sexually assaulted by the man their parents' had trusted with their well-being; all six were under the age of 10 years. Goldberg was charged with the sexual exploitation of children, six counts of performing lewd acts upon a child and two counts of possession of child pornography. Police feared he had taken photos of his disturbing actions and may have posted them on the Internet.

Goldberg was about to add yet another charge to the list: unlawful flight to avoid prosecution. After a $50,000 bond was posted and Goldberg made bail, he did what any sane criminal with some financial means would do—he fled. Somehow he managed to withdraw enough money from his U.S. bank account to provide for his needs—as much as $50,000 according to some sources. Goldberg left Long Beach, and after a quick stop at his parents' home in New Jersey, he succeeded in doing the unthinkable. He made it across the U.S. border and into Canada.

For Goldberg, a new life necessitated taking on a new name. On paper, Goldberg was now Terry Wayne Kearns, and he had a Saskatchewan birth certificate to prove it. As Goldberg settled down into a new life in Dorval, on Montréal's West Island, American authorities had elevated the suspected criminal to the dubious honour of being named to the FBI's 10 Most Wanted list.

Despite the charges Goldberg faced in the U.S. and with a pervasive illness that would continue to tempt him to perform other abuses, the fugitive was somehow able to maintain a low profile in Canada. For six long years, Goldberg's name remained on that top 10 list. For six years, FBI officials were on the hunt for a man who had allegedly destroyed the innocence of at least six young girls, and who could conceivably be preying on other unsuspecting children. And then, just as suddenly as he disappeared, the FBI in Los Angeles received a call from someone in Montréal that suspected a friend of theirs was the man they were looking for.

By now, Goldberg was entering his senior years. At 61, the fugitive might have been tired of hiding out. Perhaps he'd experienced a pang of conscience. Either way, sources suggest that Goldberg began unburdening himself to a nonprofit counsellor. He told the counsellor he was hiding out in Canada, running from the law because of charges that he believed were "trumped up." Most counsellors explain to their clients that with few exceptions, sessions between a counsellor and his or her client are confidential. Causing harm to oneself or to someone else generally falls into that exception category. So when Goldberg shared his story, you would have to believe that he knew the possible ramifications.

If the man posing as Terry Wayne Kearns had any doubt that he may have initiated a situation that could only snowball, and not in his favour, his counsellor surely dispelled that doubt. After their discussion, the counsellor logged on to the FBI's website and reviewed their most wanted list. There he was, or at least, there was a picture of the man known as Terry Wayne Kearns. When the counsellor confronted the wanted man and asked him if his name was indeed Richard Goldberg, the fugitive admitted his true identity.

The wheels of justice moved along quite rapidly from that point. An FBI agent in Ottawa was contacted, and various law enforcement personnel including the Canadian Border Services Agency and a Montréal Police SWAT team were called in to arrest Goldberg. And on Saturday, May 12, 2007, the fugitive was finally taken into custody. He likely wasn't happy with the knowledge that he'd be behind bars once again and that he'd remain there for many years to come, but Goldberg admitted he was indeed the man they were looking for and went along with the police without too much trouble.

Following an appearance before Canada's Immigration and Refugee Board, Goldberg was deported to the United States on May 24. On December 10, 2007, Goldberg faced U.S. District Judge John Walter and pleaded guilty to one count of producing child pornography. For that charge, Goldberg received a 20-year sentence, and it's not likely he'll be a free man until October 11, 2024. He is currently serving that sentence in the Federal Correctional Institution in Petersburg, Virginia.

The *America's Most Wanted* television report on Goldberg's exploits and eventual capture reported that Goldberg read a statement to the court during his sentencing. "I never did anything to be mean to anyone," he said. He went on to accuse his victims, young girls under the age of 10, of "setting him up."

As District Judge Walter said, Goldberg is truly a "deeply disturbed individual" with a "lack of remorse beyond belief." Clearly, a stroke of conscience hadn't propelled the man to tell his story.

It doesn't matter anyway. Goldberg is where he should be, and other young girls have one less predator to worry about.

Twisted Love
Allan Dwayne Schoenborn

~

*I've been looking every day for him, hiking every bush
around here looking for him. As a Merritt resident,
I'm glad he's caught. But it's a sick, shitty, friggin' story.*

–Kim Robinson, during an interview with
Kamloops Radio NL

As the self-proclaimed Country Music Capital of Canada, Merritt, BC, surrounded by the sunny hillsides and attractive lakes of the Nicola Valley, offers countless outdoor recreation opportunities. The city of about 7000 affords anyone who deigns to stop by for a while, or a lifetime, all the cultural, educational and retail amenities of city life blended seamlessly with the feel of rural living.

It is a "progressive, attractive, economically viable city that is socially responsible and environmentally sustainable," according to Merritt's mission statement—the perfect place to settle down and raise a family.

That's exactly what Darcie Clarke thought when she moved herself and her three children, Kaitlynne, 10, Max, 8, and Cordon, 5, to the area from Vancouver in the fall of 2007. New home, new community and new friends. This was their chance to start over.

Clarke had at least one, primary reason for wanting to enter a new phase in her life and move to the corner of Merritt known as Telemon Place. Surviving a stormy, 15-year-long, common-law relationship may have given her three lovely children, but it came at a significant price—a price she was no longer willing to pay.

It was true that Allan Dwayne Schoenborn, the children's father, repeatedly proclaimed his love and devotion to Clarke and their youngsters—his desire to tackle the role of doting husband and father wasn't in question. But some would call Schoenborn's temperament hot and cold. One moment, he was in a good space and life seemed promising, and the next moment, he was suspicious of Clarke's loyalties and overly protective toward the couple's children. He'd been known to blame bizarre things on Clarke, like the time he accused her of drugging the teething gel. He could be kind and thoughtful one moment and violent the next, and there was rarely a reason for his sudden changes in temperament. And most recently, he had complained that he'd been hearing voices, voices he thought were emanating from a "transmitter" in either his brain or his teeth, and these voices were making him even more anxious than usual.

Tension between the couple gained intensity in May 2007, just a few months before Clarke left Vancouver. At that time, police were called in to investigate a report of domestic violence, and their intervention resulted in Schoenborn being served with a peace bond prohibiting any contact with his estranged partner if he'd been drinking within the previous 12 hours of his visit. But even an order from the courts didn't prevent him from making poor decisions, and in August, he showed up at Clarke's house with beer and wine in a desperate attempt to convince the woman to speak with him. Clarke no longer felt safe. It seemed like the only way she'd ever be able to escape her former partner's grasp was if she moved. As the leaves were turning their vibrant fall colours, so, too, were the seasons changing in Clarke's personal life. She'd finally accepted that she needed to close that chapter in her life if she was to manage to patch up her bruised self-esteem, and so she prepared her children for the change to come.

Relocating might be one of the most stressful things a family ever has to do, but instead of being anxious, Clarke felt a welcome calm begin to settle itself in her life. As the months passed, she felt more and more at ease. For the first time in years, she could sense a measure of normalcy in her life, and it was a relief to see the children making friends and enjoying their studies at Diamond Vale Elementary School. Maybe now, Clarke must have pondered, she could finally begin to really live again.

Of course, things are rarely what they seem.

Reports are vague about exactly when Schoenborn turned up in the Nicola Valley, but it was clear that a distance of a few hundred kilometres wasn't about to keep him from his family, restraining order or not. Depending on the neighbour being questioned, it appeared that Schoenborn could have been hanging around Clarke's new home for several weeks or even months.

"He was here mostly all the time," one neighbour told a reporter with the Canadian Press in April 2008. "He hid in the house. Monday night he was raking the lawn at midnight."

But depending on the kind of encounter a person had with the man, and the length of time they might have known him, opinions about Schoenborn varied, depending on whether the person had glimpsed his idiosyncrasies or seen his seemingly softer side. Some residents remembered seeing Schoenborn shopping with Kaitlynne just days before anyone had any reason to speak with the press. On another occasion, he was spotted flying kites with Kaitlynne and her brothers. The man who raked his lawn at midnight might have been a little eccentric, but he appeared determined to lavish his children with affection.

Schoenborn's potentially violent side, on the other hand, wasn't something most of Clarke's new friends and acquaintances initially knew much about. At least some of the folks Clarke had connected with in Merritt were under the assumption that Schoenborn had been working in Vancouver, and that was why he hadn't immediately joined his family in their new home. One source told news reporters that Schoenborn said he couldn't handle working away from home any longer, and that he had decided to try to find a roofing job in the Nicola Valley area. Another person suggested that Clarke told her the couple was trying to work out their differences as a couple.

Still, it didn't take long before even new acquaintances could see that all was not well. One neighbour told reporters that provincial social workers had spoken with her about Clarke and her estranged partner. While the neighbour wouldn't elaborate on the details of the conversation, she did say she was told that Schoenborn was "very dangerous."

If the man's behaviour at his children's school was any indication, he certainly was dangerous. On one occasion, Schoenborn approached the administration and complained that one of the students had upset his daughter. When he didn't get the kind of response he was looking for, he allegedly "threatened" the nine-year-old girl in question and went on to threaten the principal as well. Schoenborn was arrested after the incident, and at a bail hearing, he told the judge, "I just have a hard time, you know, dealing with my separation of my family…it's really hard to be without the ones you love." He agreed that he hadn't handled the situation very well, but stopped short of admitting that he'd threatened anyone. "I reacted badly, I guess. But my daughter, all I saw was her tears."

The altercation at the school took place on Thursday, April 3, 2008, and was one of three episodes in which Schoenborn's behaviour resulted in his arrest; he was also arrested for being drunk in public and for an outstanding warrant for a previous offence of driving while prohibited. Any way you looked at it, no matter how long Schoenborn had actually been in the city, his questionable behaviour was starting to worry the people who lived near Darcie Clarke or had any reason to interact with the family.

Clarke also appeared to be uncertain about what to do about the situation. Perhaps it was Schoenborn's cyclic habit of being almost normal and then brooding and irritable that kept the mother confused over how to handle her relationship with her children's father. Clarke later told reporters with *The Province* that she and Schoenborn had worked out a system that seemed to appease some of his concerns over maintaining contact with the couple's youngsters. While Clarke admitted that the status between her and Schoenborn was "on again, off again," and she seemed unsure about what she wanted to do in the long term, she had arranged to visit her mother whenever Schoenborn wanted to see the children. At the very least, that bit of space provided Clarke with the time she needed to think and make a more permanent decision.

On the evening of April 4, Schoenborn had voiced his desire to do just that—spend some time with Kaitlynne, Max and Cordon that weekend. In the past, Clarke had seen Schoenborn at his worst, but that day, he didn't seem unduly agitated or behave in a way that set off any alarm bells. Schoenborn said he'd been thinking of taking the kids out to fly their kites again—what kid doesn't jump at the chance to fly a kite with their dad on a sunny spring day? It was agreed that Schoenborn would visit the children on Saturday, and Clarke decided to use the opportunity to visit her mother for the night. She then ran a few errands on Sunday morning before returning to the family's mobile home.

Life would never be the same again.

Having completed her errands, Darcie Clarke returned to her trailer home shortly before 2:00 PM on Sunday. When she entered her home, she was met by an eerie silence, but remembering Schoenborn's planned outing, Clarke likely thought her typically noisy troop just hadn't returned yet.

It's hard to imagine what must have raced through Clarke's mind when she first noticed Max and Cordon curled up together on the living room couch. They must have looked like they were sleeping. And yet that possibility was so bizarre because five- and eight-year-old boys don't willingly take a nap in the middle of a Sunday afternoon.

Clarke stood there for what probably felt like an eternity, but in actuality was but a few brief seconds. The scene swam before her in a veil of tears even before she knew for sure what her heart was telling her. And when she finally approached her two sons and touched them, they were cold. They were gone. What could have happened? What had Schoenborn done?

As horrifying as that must have been, there was still another child to consider. Kaitlynne wasn't in the room. Was it possible that she'd escaped with her life? Was it possible that Darcy still had one child to hold and love?

Rushing into the little girl's bedroom, Clarke was met with a gruesome sight. If it could be imagined, Clarke's 10-year-old daughter had suffered an even more horrifying end. There was blood everywhere, and what remained of Clarke's daughter was wrapped in the girl's favourite blanket. Schoenborn later told the court that he'd used a cleaver to kill his little girl, and that she'd kept pleading with him to forgive her before she died. But that day, standing in a sea of death and misery, her mind twisting between denial and acknowledging the reality before her and her body wracked in agony, Clarke was alone, and Schoenborn was nowhere to be found.

Dan Robins told *CBC News* that the scene outside Clarke's rental mobile home shortly after 2:00 PM on April 6 was like nothing he'd ever seen before. "The tears were just pouring. Her face was just beet red.… I've seen distraught people but, I mean, this was like a horror show."

Shortly afterward, the otherwise peaceful neighbourhood of Telemon Place was swarming with police officers, and the quiet Sunday afternoon was transposed into something that felt like a scene from *CSI*. As news of the triple murder hit the local media and spread out across the country, there was some initial speculation that Schoenborn was also dead, having committed suicide after killing his children. Twenty hours would pass before residents of Merritt and the surrounding rural area would be shocked by the news that Schoenborn was not only alive, but he was also missing. No one had any idea where the man had gone.

For residents in the area, this bit of news only added to the outrage they were already feeling over the triple murder. Now they were not only sickened by what had happened, but they also feared for the safety of their loved ones. Deadbolts were locked. Windows shut. Diamond Vale Elementary School closed its doors that Monday, and when it did reopen, it wasn't without considerable police presence monitoring lunch and recess breaks and walking the grounds while students were in school.

Nestled at the confluence of the Nicola and Coldwater rivers, the city of Merritt is somewhat unusual when compared with many other communities in British Columbia where transportation routes are sometimes limited. Merritt isn't just surrounded by the south central Interior wilderness; it is located at the entrance to the Coquihalla Highway and considered the "gateway" to several other major highways. In addition, countless logging roads diverge into the wooded hillsides, where someone who didn't want to be found could hide. And the TransCanada Highway is a mere 87 kilometres away; should a fugitive make it to that junction and land himself a ride with a passing motorist or lonely trucker, he could quite conceivably end up just about anywhere in Canada.

The RCMP and local law enforcement personnel were already facing the daunting task of finding a desperate man in the BC woods, but that didn't prevent a frustrated public and persistent media from challenging these officials about their search. Investigators were questioned about their decision to withhold information about Schoenborn being at large. That rebuff was soon followed by more specific criticisms on how officials were responding to possible sightings of the man. After all, more than 300 tips reportedly made their way into RCMP headquarters during the time Schoenborn was running scared, and to the casual observer, it was hard to know what officials were doing about the tips.

One inspector tried to quell escalating public concerns and stem a massive panic by telling the media that there were more than 60,000 police officers looking for the man who, at that time, was simply considered a "person of interest." Press releases about the case were sent to newspaper and television outlets, along with several photographs and a detailed description of Schoenborn. He was described as being 5 feet, 4 inches in height and weighing about 130 pounds, with a somewhat ruddy complexion, hazel eyes, brown hair and an unshaven face. A scar along Schoenborn's right eyebrow and down that side of his face, along with the scars on both ears, were unique markings police hoped would help a worried public in identifying the fugitive should someone happen to see him.

In the days following Schoenborn's disappearance, a helicopter equipped with thermal cameras made several sweeps of the area, looking for signs that someone might be hiding in the woods. Dog teams scoured the ground. Neighbouring provinces were also alerted, and a news release in Alberta suggested the possibility that the missing man had made it into that province. But no matter what the RCMP did, they couldn't seem to capture the missing father.

As hours turned into days, and then a week passed and Schoenborn was still on the loose, an increasingly leery public formed their own opinions about exactly where the fugitive might have taken cover. The general consensus was that he wouldn't have left the area, much less the province. Instead, there were lots of places nearby where someone could hide for an extended period of time without being detected. Jolene Lawrence, a manager working at the Stump Lake Ranch 40 minutes east of Merritt, was on board with that theory. Lawrence told reporters with the Canadian Press that there were countless areas where Schoenborn could be hiding out. "Around the Merritt area, definitely, there is a lot of forest…there are a lot of old shacks and cabins and lakes," she said.

While they were trying to cover all the possibilities, law enforcement officials seemed to agree with that local perspective. "You're talking about a very vast country. It's very easy for people to disappear in the backcountry, especially if they're equipped and they know what they're doing," Sergeant John Price of the Saanich Police Department told reporters, "…you get on a logging road and then follow the logging road until it ends and then get onto a deer trail and start walking."

It was also possible that Schoenborn was a lot more prepared for his disappearance than first thought. At that time of year, the weather in BC is mild, and the winter's blanket of snow had for the most part disappeared. There was some talk that Schoenborn had been saying he wanted to "camp out in the bush" with Van Gogh, his German shepherd–retriever cross. And then there was Schoenborn's visit to the outdoor store with Kaitlynne on the day of the murders. Was it possible that Schoenborn had premeditated the murders of his children and then planned to disappear all along?

As far as Price was concerned, if Schoenborn wanted to be found, he'd turn up eventually. Either that or he'd make it very easy for someone to find him. If, on the other hand, Schoenborn didn't want to be discovered, chances were he'd remain at large. "When you have somebody who doesn't want to be found, they're next to impossible to find," Price said. He stressed that the rural setting where this drama was playing out would only help a fugitive's chances of successfully avoiding detection, and he pointed to the case of Kitimat's Kevin Vermette as a prime example.

An increasingly frustrated public was beginning to vocalize what they thought about the situation, and they began by suggesting local law enforcement consider accepting some external help. Even days after the incident, many parents were still keeping their children home from school. People were constantly looking over their shoulders and staring at every stranger they passed to determine if maybe the person was the missing Schoenborn. "You're always looking. Every time you see something, you're thinking, 'Is that him?'" one resident told reporters. Everyone was anxious for closure. Nobody wanted another situation like what had happened in Kitimat.

One local man, Kim Robinson, believed he was the very person who could help police track down their suspect and provide his friends and neighbours with a little peace of mind. The problem was the police weren't overly enthusiastic about working with the man. In fact, they'd turned him down outright.

Robinson, a local hunter, trapper and outdoorsman, knows the backwoods surrounding Merritt better than just about anyone. He'd lived in the area for 30 years at that time, had logged the hillsides and tracked and hunted deep into the woods on a daily basis. He ran two traplines, raised cougar hounds, had bagged no less than 200 mountain lions and had come face to face with a grizzly on more than one occasion and lived to tell the tale. As far as Robinson was concerned, he believed he was the logical choice when it came to investigators tapping into the local talent to help in the search for the missing suspect.

Anyone who knew Robinson pretty much agreed with that assessment. He was held in high regard by most Merritt residents. Whether law enforcement personnel officially wanted him to be involved in the search for Schoenborn or not, Robinson spent days following the triple murder and the suspect's disappearance, scouring the backcountry he knew so well, usually accompanied by his bullmastiff, Blaze. And the one time he'd bumped into an officer during his daily treks into the bush, Robinson felt they shared a mutual respect for one another. "He was on board," Robinson told reporters from *The Province*. "He wasn't mad at me for looking."

Robinson and the RCMP never officially joined forces before the final chapter closed in the manhunt for Allan Dwayne Schoenborn. On April 16, after 10 days of being on the lam, a man walking his dog in the Hamilton Hills area of Merritt thought he might have spotted the fugitive. Noticing Robinson nearby, the man—who was known in the media only as "Pat"—waved the trapper over and shared his suspicions. Robinson tracked Schoenborn to a patch of grass near the town's tourist-information centre, about two kilometres southeast of Merritt. "He looked like a little bastard that hadn't eaten for 10 days," Robinson later told reporters.

It's unclear if Schoenborn had been in the area, which wasn't far from the scene of the triple murder, during the entire 10 days he spent avoiding the authorities, or if he'd moved around from place to place. But one thing was certain—Schoenborn was done. He was a beaten soul who by that point probably wanted to be found. When Robinson, whose own son described him as a "mountain of a man," found what Robinson characterized as a "hurting unit," he was passed out on the grass. Alerted to Robinson's presence by his protective dog, Van Gogh, Schoenborn tried to get up. Robinson told Schoenborn to sit down. Schoenborn asked Robinson if he was going to kill him. Robinson said no, then tied Schoenborn to a tree, called the police and waited for them to arrive.

As news of the capture started to trickle through the social fabric of Merritt and the surrounding area, eventually hitting the evening news, there was a collective sigh of relief. Finally, people could unlock their doors and send their children back to school without worry. The man who police suspected of killing his three children had been apprehended and was spending his first of, hopefully, many nights behind bars.

There was considerable pride over Schoenborn's arrest, and Robinson played a key role in apprehending the man. "[Kim is] the best there is at that, at tracking and that stuff," long-time acquaintance Sandra Nelson told reporters with the Canadian Press and the *Globe and Mail*. "And that's just the way Kim is. He'd do it for the community mainly, for the safety of everybody involved, including Allan [Schoenborn] himself...just to bring the whole thing to a happy ending, as happy as it could be, and for the safety of the community and everything else."

Robinson's son, Paul, 27, said he was proud of his father and wasn't at all surprised that his dad had rounded up the missing man. "If anyone was going to find [Schoenborn], it was him," Paul told reporters. "It's his livelihood. It's something he's interested in doing...he believes in truth and justice and doing the right thing."

While Robinson appeared to be a take-charge kind of person who felt driven to use his skills to help find Schoenborn, he was not of a vigilante temperament. The level-headed Robinson knew quite well that while Schoenborn was a suspect, no one knew at that point in the sordid saga if the man was actually guilty or not. Although he was always ready to protect himself if the need arose, Robinson didn't use unnecessary force in any situation. When the police arrived at the scene, Robinson pointed to Schoenborn, reportedly said, "I'm out of here," and left the officers to do their work.

If Allan Dwayne Schoenborn looked to be in rough shape before his 10-day wilderness excursion, it was nothing compared to what he looked like when Robinson finally captured him. The already small man seemed to have withered even more. Schoenborn was weak and dehydrated. He had several cuts of various depths on one arm, suggesting that he had tried repeatedly to kill himself, though speculation varied on that theory. He was too weak to walk and was initially transported to the hospital for treatment before being taken to the local police detachment.

Now that Schoenborn, the only suspect in the triple slaying, had been apprehended, an angry public was anxious to hear directly from the man at the centre of the story. At the same time, people questioned what some felt were serious flaws in the criminal justice system. After the incident at the school in which he had threatened a nine-year-old girl and the school principal, Schoenborn had been jailed and subsequently released on bail, and the public wanted to know why. Even the Merritt police had questioned the decision to release Schoenborn, saying there would be "public outrage."

Aside from the story about Schoenborn's violent outburst at the school, RCMP spokeswoman Constable Annie Linteau told a news conference that during a bail hearing conducted over the telephone, the court was presented with a checklist filled out by one of the officers involved in that incident and the arrest that followed. The checklist highlighted several concerns, including the fact that Schoenborn had a criminal record for violent offences in the past. Thanks to the plethora of media reports, Schoenborn's past acts were well documented and easily accessible to area residents. It was clear to everyone involved that the public would be shocked should the man be released.

Merritt RCMP also voiced concerns during the bail hearing, stating that Schoenborn was a possible flight risk, and they didn't think he'd make his scheduled court date on April 7. The suggestion seemed to provoke near disbelief in Schoenborn. According to the transcript of the bail hearing, Schoenborn argued that he was a "responsible adult just trying to work my way back home.... I've got a grade nine education, I've worked all my life as a roofer. I am not very good with words, but I don't understand how he would—he would—he could come to that conclusion that I may flee from my family."

Although Justice of the Peace Fraser Hodge admitted to having "grave reservations" about releasing Schoenborn, in the end the bail request was approved. Perhaps Justice Hodge thought Schoenborn deserved another chance, but his decision rocked everyone involved. Surely the justice of the peace had been presented with the evidence required to warrant some time behind bars for the desperate father—at least enough evidence to keep him there until he could appear before a judge the following week.

And there was more. Not long before the murders took place, Schoenborn had pleaded guilty to violating a protection order that outlined strict conditions surrounding any contact he might wish to have with Clarke. It appeared that Justice Hodge hadn't been provided with that bit of information. Perhaps if he had, it would have been the added ammunition he needed for his reservations to outweigh his desire to give the distraught Schoenborn another chance.

Schoenborn's release from custody after the school incident irked Merritt residents, but police were also under fire for waiting so long to inform the community that he was alive and at large following the triple murder. Parents of young children were especially concerned. "We don't know if he's around our back door," Brenda Gustafson, the young mother of a 22-month-old child said during a community meeting held on April 10. "We're scared to go out. We're scared to go downtown. We're scared to go anywhere."

Investigators had tried to reassure the nervous community by explaining the various steps they'd been taking to track Schoenborn. They also asked residents to identify and report anything they might consider out of the ordinary. RCMP assistant commissioner Al Macintyre told a press conference on April 10 that there were 30 investigators on the case and looking for Schoenborn at any given time. He also told the public that if "you find that the rusted-out pickup in the back 40 is suddenly gone…or find the door to your summer cabin kicked open, we want to know." On the other hand, the officers' allegedly slow response in checking out several reports of potential sightings of the man—in one case a witness swore she saw Schoenborn returning some empties—was also criticized.

Sadly, any analysis of the situation couldn't turn back the clock and change what had happened. If Schoenborn hadn't been released on bail, his children would likely still be alive. As David Laird, Merritt's mayor at the time, told reporters, Schoenborn's capture was the best possible news under the circumstances, and that everyone had worked together to make Schoenborn's arrest a reality. "There will be further investigations, inquiries and coroner's reports and we will leave that to the professionals and allow due process to take place."

It was a first step toward closure and healing—but not before a curious public learned what Schoenborn had to say in his defence. Even though he was in custody, he was still only a suspect. It was time that the world heard from Allan Dwayne Schoenborn.

"I don't know where to start or where to end for that matter." Those were the first words Schoenborn wrote in a June 12, 2008, letter addressed to Darcie Clarke. The letter was read into evidence on Tuesday, October 12, 2009, during Schoenborn's trial, and later released and reprinted in the *Kamloops Daily News*. Schoenborn's words weave a convoluted tale that could only be attributed to a disturbed mind. Up until that point, Schoenborn had pleaded not guilty to the murder of his three children. It was inconceivable to anyone involved with the case that the man had the audacity to do so. But with the release of his letter and the words of a face-to-face interview Schoenborn had with Clarke during a prison visit on June 30, an increasingly saddened public now had a glimpse into what was going on in Schoenborn's mind that fateful day in April.

Although it didn't make what happened to the children any easier to bear, it did provide the court with a "reason" for the crime, albeit a psychotic one.

According to Schoenborn's various statements, the misguided father was convinced that his children were being molested. He said he knew there was nothing he could do to keep them safe, so he decided to take matters into his own hands. What follows is part of the transcript of Schoenborn's visit with Clarke:

Schoenborn: Darc, (sighs) I, I thought they were bein' molested.

Clarke: (sniffs) No.

Schoenborn: An' I thought, it came over in a drove, in one big commotion in my back of my brain, it just flooded. An' I just seen, I di—there's nothin' I can do. It's been goin' on for some time. An' it just came on in one big flood. An' I realized there's nothin' I can do about it, no matter how hard I try.

Clarke: No.

Schoenborn: So, I put 'em where they'll be safe.

Clarke: (sniffs)

Schoenborn: And stay young an' innocent.

When Clarke confronted Schoenborn with the fact that he'd tortured his children, Schoenborn denied the accusation. He said he had no intention of torturing them but admitted that things didn't "go quick" like he had planned. "Not like I knew what I was doing," he added.

According to his letter, and various other statements, Schoenborn said that he hadn't planned on being alive to explain anything to Clarke, much less a court of law. It was his full intention to "[go] with them…Darcie, I hope now you can see I was not running from my doing or police. I was running toward my children. Lord Jesus knows how I tried to get to them. I hope knowing this helps through some of the longer days and nights."

His letter goes on to tell how, during his 10 days on the lam, he made one gash after another on his wrists until there were "17 gashes, big and small." Although each gash was deep enough to bleed, the blood would eventually stop flowing. Realizing he wasn't being very successful at slashing his wrists, Schoenborn went on to explain how he'd considered other methods of finishing his "quest towards the children," including the idea of jumping "in front of a moving truck or starvation," and how he'd abandoned each of them for one reason or another.

Then suddenly, everything changed. "As you can tell I'm not able to think straight," Schoenborn wrote. "Somewhere about here my priorities change from our children, over to you and to eating…By Day 8 or 9, all was secondary to eating."

When Schoenborn finally went to trial in the fall of 2009, he never pleaded guilty to charges of first-degree murder in the deaths of Kaitlynne, Max and Cordon. He did, however, acknowledge that he was responsible for their deaths, and during his trial, he explained his actions in gruesome detail. He said that after he hugged Max, he'd noticed the smell of semen in his hair, and that confirmed for him that his kids were indeed being molested.

"After smelling Maxie I came to the realization this wasn't in my head," he told the court. "I did it for the right reasons. I did it for them. I gave my children up to be in a better place."

Schoenborn then explained how he used a cleaver to kill Kaitlynne first. "She may have put her hand up. She said, 'I'm sorry, Dad.' I swung again." He said he used a pillow to smother Cordon, thinking it would be faster, but Schoenborn admitted it took about five minutes before Cordon's chest heaved for the last time.

After two lengthy kills, Schoenborn thought a plastic bag over the head would be a quicker way to kill Max. "He fought me, he fought me. I told him it was daddy, 'shhh.' He settled down right after I said that. He was still there, he heard me. Maxie was about two minutes."

In one final, strange act of what some might perceive as remorse, Schoenborn placed the brothers together on the couch. He then took Kaitlynne's lifeless body to the bathroom, cleaned her up, and wrapped her in that favourite blanket on her bed. When he was finished describing his actions, his attorney asked him if he did the right thing.

"Yes, I did."

Even a layperson could see the direction in which Schoenborn's lawyers were headed, and Dr. Roy O'Shaughnessy was backing their efforts. The psychiatrist testified to the BC Supreme Court that he believed Schoenborn was in a psychotic state at the time of the murders, and that the man earnestly believed he was performing an act of kindness for his children. "The distortions in the thinking led him to believe—I think probably at a moment's notice at the time of their deaths—that the only way to protect them was, in fact, to kill them and put them in heaven," the Canadian Press reported of O'Shaughnessy's testimony. "In his disillusioned view of the world, it was logical."

The prosecution did not agree with the defence's plans that suggested Schoenborn was somehow not responsible for his actions because of a mental deficiency. The prosecution argued that Schoenborn's actions were "intentional and planned," and that they were likely fuelled by a desire for revenge against his estranged partner. The Crown's psychiatrist further challenged O'Shaughnessy's assessment of Schoenborn's state of mind, saying it was "impossible to tell precisely what his state of mind was" at the time of the murders.

If the public had experienced any sense of relief that Schoenborn was behind bars, there was a growing concern that the man who had once been one of Canada's most wanted fugitives wouldn't remain in jail for very long.

As it turned out, those fears were well founded. On February 22, 2010, after listening to arguments from both sides for three long months, BC Supreme Court Justice Robert Powers decided that, "on balance of probabilities [Schoenborn] was suffering from a disease of the mind." Schoenborn was found guilty of killing his children, but "not criminally responsible" for their deaths.

With the verdict handed down, Schoenborn would have to appear in front of the British Columbia Review Board, whose responsibility it is to "protect public safety while also safeguarding the rights and freedoms of mentally disordered persons who are alleged to have committed an offence." Schoenborn would eventually be placed at the Forensic Psychiatric Institute in Port Coquitlam, a facility specializing in treatment and services for "adults with mental illness who are in conflict with the law."

Public perception of the Schoenborn case varied widely from shock and outrage that the man would not be sentenced to jail time, to frustration over the lack of help and services available to people with mental health issues. But the biggest shock likely came on April 6, 2010, exactly two years to the day after the Schoenborn children were murdered and less than two months after the end of the man's trial—he approached the BC Review Board asking for a conditional discharge. The Canadian Press reported that Schoenborn told the review panel he wanted to be released so he could "get work building houseboats along the Fraser River."

Schoenborn also tried to prevent Clarke from presenting a victim impact statement, saying it would likely be "hysterical." His request was denied, and Darcie Clarke addressed the panel through a written statement: "I will not be safe if Allan gets out. He will come looking for me and my family."

It appears the panel agreed. Although the psychiatric facility is about "treatment and rehabilitation…not punishment," their assessment of Schoenborn's state of mind was without prejudice. Dr. Johann Brink was Schoenborn's psychiatrist, as well as the director of clinical services where Schoenborn is currently being held. Dr. Brink testified that while Schoenborn's behaviour had improved, "…in terms of his understanding of his illness, his plans, his willingness to accept treatment, and in terms of the index offences and their gravity, the accused continues to lack insight."

Although Dr. Brink has yet to "refine" Schoenborn's diagnosis, "he is clear that the accused is suffering from a psychotic disorder, likely a delusional disorder. [Schoenborn] also has historic substance abuse disorders and presents with a paranoid personality disorder, the implications of which have yet to be assessed."

In the end, Schoenborn's attempt to secure freedom was denied by the psychiatric panel hearing his request, saying that Schoenborn continued to pose a significant risk to the public. Furthermore, he was ordered "to have no access to the community, even under escort." The panel also prohibited any contact between Schoenborn and Darcie Clarke. Schoenborn will remain secluded and undergo treatment on the secure A2 ward of the hospital.

Schoenborn reportedly didn't appreciate everything that was said during the hearing, but he appeared at peace with the panel's final verdict, saying that he thought they "decided right for me and the community."

For Schoenborn and Clarke and their extended family, life has changed forever. The same holds true for the people of Merritt. Hunter, trapper and wilderness tracker Kim Robinson once told Kamloops Radio NL that everyone involved was glad Schoenborn had been caught and brought to justice, but that didn't change the fact that it was "a sick, shitty, friggin' story."

Part Three

HISTORICAL CASES

~

In the age of modern media, all we need to do is turn on the television to hear about the latest notable happenings in our neighbourhoods or across the world. If we miss the supper hour newscast, we can google our favourite broadcaster and read copies of their leading stories or choose any one of countless other options for information gathering. With all this at our fingertips, there's no reason why we can't be aware of current events, we only need the desire to know.

The same wasn't true 100 or so years ago. Communities just 12 kilometres away from each other might not be aware of imminent news unfolding close enough to quite possibly affect them. It took an event of momentous proportions for information to travel quickly over any great distance, but when that critical, significant event did take place, news would spread one way or another, and word of mouth was often the most effective method of transportation.

Indubitably, there were always significant events that outshone all the others, and these stories spread like wildfire without the aid of modern technology. That was especially true when it came to the world of crime. Even with a sparse population covering an entire country, when a lone, gun-slinging, whiskey-guzzling, thumb-your-nose-at-the-law kind of guy was moving through town, people knew about it, sometimes before he even got there. And despite the vast emptiness that was the Wild West, most of these criminals met their maker in a stand-off with the law.

Two of Canada's more outlandish historic criminal sagas are most certainly the stories of the Donnelly family and the Mad Trapper. In the case of the Donnellys, several members of the family were underhanded in their business and personal interactions and were wanted by the law at one time or another. But even a criminal doesn't deserve to see his loved ones butchered. The people responsible for murdering five members of this notorious family were never brought to justice.

When it comes to the Mad Trapper, well, that's another story entirely. Although the Mounties captured their man in this instance, they were never successful in actually identifying him. As far as history is concerned, the Mad Trapper is still a wanted man, at least with regards to discovering his real name.

Rat River Recluse Still Eludes Authorities, Even After Death
ALBERT JOHNSON

~

...the dynamite did practically no damage to the cabin, and it wasn't until after Johnson had [later] escaped [that] the cabin was destroyed by manual labour, so that Johnson could not return and again use it as a so-called fort.

–from a 1932 report penned by Constable William Carter as it appears in *The Mad Trapper: Unearthing a Mystery* by Barbara Smith

JANUARY 1940

The clerk sorted through a box of personal effects, logging each item in the small collection. After almost a decade in storage, one glass bottle with five pearls, valued at about $15, and five fragments of gold dental work worth about $3.20, were being sent to the Public Administrator, as was a second small, glass bottle containing about $9.36 worth of alluvial gold.

The Savage 30-30 rifle, model number 99, was destined for the RCMP Police Museum in Regina, Saskatchewan, along

RAT RIVER RECLUSE STILL ELUDES AUTHORITIES
ALBERT JOHNSON

with one altered 16-gauge Ivor Johnson shotgun; a 22-calibre Winchester rifle, model number 58, also altered; a pocket compass; an axe; a pair of handmade snowshoes; and a sack containing a lard tin and lid that were once used for making tea.

There was more: assorted boxes of shotgun shells, rifle covers, swatches of moose hide, salt and pepper, twine, scraps of metal and wire, a Gillette safety razor, fish hooks, nails, pills and matches. These items, though once precious assets to a shrewd outdoorsman, were considered "articles of no value" and eventually tossed unceremoniously into the Ottawa River. Perhaps there was some significance to the action at the time when these items were sent off to their various locations, but that significance has been lost. In any case, these few personal effects, along with $2140 in cash—the entire estate of one Albert Johnson—were once loaded into a backpack and carried across the Arctic tundra in what was perhaps the most bizarre manhunt in Canadian history.

And yet not one of these personal items told anything about who this man was and why an ordinary visit from the Royal Canadian Mounted Police (RCMP) propelled Johnson into the history books as one of Canada's most wanted criminals.

Constable Edgar Millen was performing little more than a routine call when he stopped by to check in on a newcomer to the arctic wilderness near Fort McPherson, Northwest Territories, on July 21, 1931. Inspector Alexander Neville Eames, commander of the Western Arctic subdivision of the RCMP had asked Millen to find out about a newcomer going by the name of Albert Johnson after Anglican Bishop W.A. Geddes overheard some concerns about the man.

A few years earlier, locals who had lived in the north for generations noticed that more and more new faces were moving into the area. Eccentric individuals had always been attracted to the solitude offered by living in such a remote location, but the desire for solitude typically only accounted for the rare individual trickling in from time to time. Now, things were changing. People, most often single men, were coming to the North for a different reason—money.

On October 29, 1929, the world experienced an economic disaster without precedent. On "Black Tuesday," as economists and historians later referred to that date, Wall Street crashed as stocks plummeted in value, setting off a domino effect felt the world over. That event, coupled with the drought Canada was experiencing, meant people were out of work. After years of nearly nonexistent rain, the country's dry and barren prairies could no longer produce adequate crops. Farmers hoping to make money to feed their families migrated to cities in search of jobs, but many couldn't find work. The unemployment rate skyrocketed, and even the most capable of men were queuing up in breadlines or vying for a handout at soup kitchens.

Under those conditions, the North represented possible relief. The men who migrated there to make money hoped to achieve some modicum of success in the fur trade or perhaps try their hand at mining for gold. The idea was to set up a temporary camp, live off the land and return home once they'd earned enough to pay the bills.

The problem was that many of the newcomers vastly underestimated the hardships and struggles of northern living, and authorities worried that should these newcomers find themselves in danger because of a lack of knowledge or the inability to deal with those struggles, it could also put others at risk, especially their would-be rescuers. It therefore fell to the RCMP to make sure new residents were equipped, both physically and mentally, for life in the North, as well as ensuring that they possessed the necessary skills to meet the challenges before them.

On that July afternoon, it was Millen's job to make sure Johnson knew what was in store for him and to perhaps find out a little bit of information about the man in the process. From what Millen understood, Johnson struck most people as a bit of an enigma. To anyone who ventured to ask, Johnson was tight-lipped about who he was and where he'd come from. His actions, however, provided locals with at least an opinion on the man.

Johnson had apparently landed about five kilometres from Fort McPherson woefully ill equipped, floating along the Peel River in a makeshift raft composed of three tightly bound logs. Abandoning his raft, Johnson walked from there into town.

It appeared that he hadn't travelled with any supplies and didn't have much of anything on his person aside from his clothes. But it was soon evident that money was not a problem for the stranger, and he certainly knew what to do with the considerable amount of cash he was carrying—it seemed that Johnson hadn't wandered north because he didn't have the means to live somewhere else. His first stop was at the Northern Traders Limited store, where he purchased a 16-gauge, single-barrel Ivor Johnson shotgun and 25 shells. He then stopped at the Hudson's Bay trading post and spared no expense to ensure he had all the supplies he needed. Finally, Johnson purchased a canoe from a local named Abe Francis—he'd need a well-built and sturdy vessel to manage his way along the Husky River to the mouth of the Rat River and down its winding and challenging waterway.

Although sources differ, it appears that Millen first met with Johnson at his campsite, just outside Fort McPherson. With practised precision that came from years of police work, Millen made a mental note of the man's appearance. Johnson's hair was light brown, and anyone who saw him remembered how it "grew in tufts." He had blue eyes, a "snubbed, upturned nose" and was noted to have "moderate prominence of cheek bones; ears definitely lobed; loww-set [sic] and close to head." Millen estimated that Johnson was between 35 and 40 years of age.

Johnson was about 5 feet, 10 inches in height and weighed about 170 pounds, making him of average build. And although

Johnson was well covered, Millen could tell the man packed a lot of strength beneath his several layers of clothing. In time, Johnson proved that he could haul supplies weighing as much as 200 pounds, manoeuvre his canoe in the roughest waters and snowshoe heavily laden over snow-covered mountains.

After a brief introduction, Millen asked Johnson where he was from and what he was planning to do in that neck of the woods. Johnson replied that he'd spent the summer of 1930 on the prairies and had travelled into the area via the Mackenzie River system. He told Millen he intended to settle down along the banks of the Rat River, roughly 32 kilometres west of their current location, and perhaps establish his own trapline there. If that didn't pan out the way he'd like, he might even move farther on to the Yukon. When Millen asked why he seemed to have arrived so woefully unprepared for his expedition, Johnson explained that he'd lost his gear and was in the process of outfitting himself once again.

Johnson's story raised some suspicions in Millen's mind because, before Millen had even met the man, he had learned that Johnson arrived on the Peel River and not the Mackenzie as Johnson had indicated. Still, Millen didn't press the issue. Nor did he ask for more specific information. Millen knew the North attracted all kinds of loners who kept to themselves and guarded their privacy for any number of reasons. So after ensuring that Johnson was indeed properly equipped and reminding him that he'd need to purchase a hunting licence if he was planning to trap in the area, the officer proceeded on his way to tend to his other duties.

Shortly after their brief meeting, Johnson bought the remaining supplies he needed, packed his canoe and headed out for what was to become his new home—at least for a short time.

Johnson chose well when it came to selecting a location to dig in and set down a foundation for what some sources referred to as a small but strongly reinforced fortress. The site along the Rat River where Johnson squatted was about 24 kilometres up from a section of the river named "Destruction City," in recognition of the powerful rapids that had destroyed a small army's worth of canoes and men over the years.

Once he chose the site, Johnson dug a one-metre deep, 2.5-by-3.5-metre foundation among a stand of trees, bordered on three sides by the winding river. He then constructed a log framework that rose up 1.5 metres from ground level in the front and about one metre in the back, with a flat roof sloping from front to back. Spaces between the logs were filled with sod and mud, and a sod roof added insulation against the cold. A second, shorter wall about 0.5 metres high reinforced the wall facing the river, presumably to act as a buffer against the wind and elements. The entire cabin had but one small window and a door scarcely large enough for Johnson to wedge his way through.

Rat River Recluse Still Eludes Authorities
Albert Johnson

His home was creatively built using the minimal supplies available, but it was also solid enough to withstand the arctic weather and just about anything else life was planning to toss its way.

That Johnson was a smart and resourceful man was immediately evident to whomever he met. He was also a cautious man, preparing for any eventuality to such an extent that he stored some of his supplies in what's referred to as a "stage cache"—a platform suspended from a nearby tree.

When he had finished building his home and storing supplies, Johnson settled in to the next task—developing a routine. For the next six months, he traversed the hillsides, set traps and pretty much kept his own company. Most folks respected a person's need for privacy, but even in a land where solitary individuals are commonplace, there are limits.

Among trappers in the wild North, there is an unspoken code of conduct that most naturally abide by, a kind of common respect that is automatically given. These rugged men living in the bush were reclusive by nature. They weren't much for socializing and, like Johnson, were naturally withdrawn. Still, there was such a thing as being neighbourly, especially when it came to greeting the Aboriginal trappers in the area, on whose traditional homelands people like Johnson were treading. It was quite common for First Nations peoples to stop by on occasion to exchange pleasantries and perhaps even share a cup of tea and a bit of sustenance before moving on.

In a report later penned by RCMP Constable William Carter, it appeared that Johnson had no intention of sharing tea and goodies with anyone. When some of these trappers decided to stop by and meet the newcomer, Johnson greeted them with a gun pointed at their faces and stern instructions to move on. He wasn't about to turn his cabin into a cafeteria where idle chitchat reigned at his expense. This, of course, didn't sit well with Johnson's Aboriginal neighbours, but his actions ensured the solitude he craved.

At least for a while.

William Vittrekwa, William Nerysoo and Jacob Drymeat had tried to say hello to the reclusive Johnson, only to be told in no uncertain terms that he didn't want visitors. Not impressed with the newcomer's attitude, or with having a gun pointed at their faces, the three men reported the incident to the RCMP. It's uncertain if Johnson's behaviour was their only complaint, or if there was indeed merit to the suggestion that the man might have been interfering with the Aboriginal hunters' traps. In any case, the men also reported that since Johnson had moved into the area, the three men had all noticed their traps had been tripped and hung on nearby trees on several occasions. It was something that hadn't happened in the past, and if it continued, it could prove to be a serious problem because trapping and selling animal pelts was how these men earned a living.

In retrospect, it is strange that a man who wanted nothing more than to be left alone would do something that would so obviously raise the ire of his neighbours and bring him the attention he so clearly wanted to avoid. Either way, as soon as the disgruntled trappers gave Constable Millen a brief description of the man, the officer immediately knew that they were talking about the same man he had met and interviewed just a few months earlier.

It was time Mr. Johnson received another visit from the RCMP. This time, Millen intended his constables to collect a little more information about the mystery man.

Constable Alfred W. King and Special Constable Joseph Bernard, Millen's entire complement of officers at the Arctic Red River RCMP Post, were dispatched to check on Albert Johnson on December 26, 1931. It took the better part of Boxing Day for King and Bernard to mush their dog team from the RCMP post to Fort McPherson in temperatures that dipped to −34°C. That first night, they stayed with John Firth, a Hudson's Bay trader known for hosting elaborate parties from time to time, and Firth suggested that the men return for the fete he was planning that New Year's Eve. With the added incentive of a grand evening, King and Bernard finished the majority of their 128-kilometre trek the next day and spent the night camped a short distance from Johnson's cabin. They intended to approach the man in the morning, discuss the complaint and remind Johnson that he needed to purchase a trapping licence if he intended to hunt, and then return to Fort McPherson.

As they approached the cabin, the constables noticed smoke from the chimney and a pair of snowshoes propped against the wall. Johnson was obviously home.

King repeatedly knocked on the door. He introduced himself through the wooden barrier separating him from the man inside, explaining that he only wanted to talk. But his efforts were met with nothing more than silence. Johnson didn't say a word—he didn't even tell the officer to go away. Johnson's passive-aggressive behaviour was hostile and unsettling, and King could only suppose that the man either hated the police or was mentally unstable. After an hour of persistent requests, King and Bernard retreated to their sled and decided to carry on to Aklavik and speak with Inspector Eames at RCMP headquarters about the matter.

On learning of the complaint and hearing about his men's experience, Eames shared King and Bernard's concerns. Johnson wasn't just a reticent loner, he'd demonstrated a distinct lack of respect for authority, and that, Eames conjectured, smacked of aggression. It was imperative they look into the matter and ensure that Johnson wasn't a danger to himself or others.

The inspector sent King and Bernard back to Johnson's cabin with a search warrant enabling them to break into the cabin if necessary in order to confront the man. Eames also dispatched Constable Robert G. McDowell and Special Constable Lazarus Sittichiulis as backup, along with rifles and sidearms and enough supplies to camp overnight.

When the foursome arrived at the cabin on the morning of December 31, the same smoky chimney greeted them and the snowshoes were still propped against the wall. It was clear that however irritated Johnson might have been at King's earlier visit, it certainly hadn't pushed Johnson into leaving his cabin.

The officers were about to learn how determined Johnson was to keep his distance and just how dangerous a man he was.

McDowell, Bernard and Sittichiulis stayed back as King made his way up the riverbank to Johnson's front door. As King was trudging up to the cabin, he shouted Johnson's name, saying that if he didn't cooperate, King had a search warrant and would force his way into the building. Once at the cabin, King reached out to knock on the door.

Johnson never said a word. Instead, he let his 30-30 do the talking for him.

The man that people would eventually call the "Mad Trapper" fired directly through the cabin door, and the bullet hit its target full on. King fell to the ground, his body searing with pain, and yet the officer knew he couldn't give up. He needed to gather every ounce of strength he still had to haul himself away from the cabin and to safer ground.

As King dragged himself around to the side of the cabin and then pulled himself up enough to stagger to the shelter of some nearby trees, the three officers he'd left behind rushed to his aid and began pummelling Johnson's cabin with bullets.

At that point, their focus was on distracting Johnson and getting King some medical attention. Bullets flew everywhere; one narrowly missing McDowell. Fortunately, King managed to get to the embankment and roll toward the river. Rushing to King's side, the officers knew right away that King's injuries were life threatening. If the blood on his jacket was any indication, he had taken a bullet to the chest.

If the fallen officer had any chance of survival, he had to get to a hospital as quickly as possible. The problem was that the men would have to travel back to Aklavik to get the medical help King required, and it usually took a full two days to cover the 128 kilometres via dog team. The officers were pretty sure King wouldn't hold up for 48 hours; they would have to push the dogs harder than they'd ever worked in their lives.

Sled dogs love to run. Sometimes it seems as if they can't get enough of it, even after lengthy journeys lasting several days. Still, pushing the dogs to mush flat out for 128 kilometres straight after already working for half a day to get to Johnson's cabin, and doing so with temperatures hovering at −40°C and against the stinging wind, the whole challenge seemed impossible. McDowell and his colleagues would have to use every ounce of cunning and experience to get the most out of the sled dogs.

The three Mounties navigated the two-day trip in 20 hours, despite the 20-knot winds that hampered their progress. One dog died of exhaustion during the trip, but their injured colleague was still alive when the group pulled into Aklavik at seven o'clock on the morning of January 1, 1932. Dr. J.A. Urguhart examined King and found that the bullet had passed through his body, from the left side of his chest to the right, missing all the major organs along its path. King would survive his ordeal.

Sadly, King's experience was only the first scene in a story that continued to play out for weeks, and with even more drastic consequences.

While King was recovering in the hospital, his colleagues geared up for a more aggressive approach to dealing with the recluse of Rat River. Johnson had proved that he wasn't just a stubborn loner; he was resourceful and dangerous. Now, instead of the police simply wanting to speak with him about a misdemeanour, they were after him for attempted murder.

Officers were also starting to wonder if Johnson had a criminal record somewhere. They knew next to nothing about the man, but from what they'd learned when dealing with other criminals, Johnson's behaviour seemed to indicate an intense hatred for the law.

Recognizing Johnson as a more formidable opponent than even Eames had originally thought, the inspector began to put plans in motion for another confrontation. This time, Eames equipped seven men. Eames, the men and their supplies would be hauled by two large dog teams—a huge force of mushers that was necessary when one considered the amount of supplies required to set up camp and feed everybody, not to mention the additional firearms and ammunition they might need to take down their adversary.

Led by Eames, the posse left Aklavik on January 4. By the evening of the following day, before they even had the chance to approach Johnson, supplies were already running low. In particular, they needed more dog food—with temperatures remaining in the −40°C range, the dogs needed more fuel than usual to keep up the pace they were asked to set. While purchasing supplies at a trading post at the mouth of the Husky River, Eames added a little extra firepower to his already extensive arsenal of weapons—nine kilograms of dynamite. If explosives didn't put an end to this ridiculous interchange between Johnson and the authorities, Eames wasn't quite sure what would.

One source explained that before heading out to Johnson's place, the team waited for an Aboriginal guide named Charlie Rat to join the group. Local First Nations peoples frequently worked alongside the RCMP, acting as guides and translators and sometimes serving as special constables in situations like this one where knowledge of the landscape and a strong ability to deal with the elements were vital to the success of a mission. Rat was asked to lead the group to the back of Johnson's cabin.

Finally, on January 9, the group surrounded Johnson's bunker. They were surprised to find that Johnson had not fled his home in the intervening eight days since he'd shot King. Smoke still spilled out of the chimney, and the man's snowshoes still leaned against the cabin wall. Defiant to the end, Johnson wasn't about to give up easily.

As Eames approached the cabin and hollered for Johnson, his men were ready with their rifles loaded and aimed. Eames told the man that he wasn't wanted for murder since King had survived his ordeal. But the inspector added that the cabin was surrounded by officers and that they weren't planning to leave without Johnson in tow.

Johnson didn't waste his breath on a reply. Eames' words were met by nothing but silence.

Eames and his officers continued to move toward the cabin, unsure what to think. Suddenly, Johnson seemed to fire in every direction. He had watched the men approach, and once they were close enough that Johnson had clear aim, he began his attack. He had several weapons positioned through hollows he'd made in the cabin walls, giving him the distinct advantage of being able to shoot from each side of his home even though he'd only built in a single window.

The officers responded to Johnson's aggression, repeatedly firing rounds of their own. However, that did nothing to dissuade the man; it may have only added to the adrenalin rush he might have felt at that moment. Finally, Eames decided to get out the dynamite.

It seemed logical to think that the added firepower would give Eames and his men an edge in this ongoing battle, but the dynamite had to be thawed out first. The only safe way to do that was to use the officers' body heat, placing the explosives near their skin or under their arms. Once the dynamite thawed, the officers wended their way as close to the cabin as possible, lit the fuses and hurled the dynamite at their target. In the end, all they managed to do was burn a lot of calories and blow up a lot of dynamite. The extreme cold dampened the dynamite's power, and Johnson's cabin sat undamaged despite their efforts.

By now, Eames and his team were exhausted and frozen. They couldn't take shelter from the elements, which was an advantage Johnson certainly had. They were running low on supplies, and they were getting discouraged—how could one man defend himself so completely from a bevy of trained guides and lawmen? Still, they had one more plan to execute before they had to retreat. With any luck, this last attack might snuff out their foe.

It was now three o'clock in the morning. Eames bundled together the remaining sticks of dynamite and arranged a single fuse. He then asked Knut Lang, the tallest member of his team, to run toward Johnson's cabin until he thought he was close enough to throw the dynamite where it might do some actual damage.

Sources differ about what happened next. Some suggest the dynamite fell onto the sod roof and blew up, reducing the cabin to a heap of splintered wood. An official report later penned by Constable William Carter, one of the members of the team working that day, suggested that the blast barely dented the roof, let alone destroyed Johnson's stronghold. In either case, Johnson didn't respond to the explosion until officers began to move toward the cabin once again, apparently expecting to find him either injured or dead. Johnson was neither. He was, however, as angry as ever.

When the officers attempted to shine a light into the cabin to check on the man's condition, Johnson fired once again, blasting the flashlight bulb. It was clear that Johnson wasn't going to surrender under any circumstances; the battle was evolving into a situation of kill or be killed. It was equally clear that Eames and his men had used up most of their arsenal and were getting increasingly low on supplies.

Cold and tired, it was time for the officers to pull back and regroup.

On January 14, after he returned to the Aklavik detachment, Eames contacted Constable Millen, asking him to return to Johnson's cabin and assess the damage while Eames began pulling together another team. Working with a local tracker named Karl Garlund, Millen made it to Johnson's cabin on January 16. This time, no smoke rose from the chimney. This time, the snowshoes were gone. Johnson had fled.

If Johnson was a wanted man before, he was now a fugitive on the run with a vast wilderness in which to hide.

On Eames' orders, Millen and Garlund waited at Johnson's cabin; another group of seven men were expected to arrive by dog team at any time. With every attempt to flush out the reclusive eccentric, the officers had equipped themselves with more and more firepower. This time their arsenal included several homemade bombs. But they needed more than a collection of powerful weapons. What they really needed at that moment was for the snow to stop falling. It was already impossible to pick up Johnson's tracks because they were buried under a heavy blanket of snow. Before proceeding in any direction, the team had to speculate which direction Johnson might go. They then had to travel against the blinding snow and biting wind and do so mostly in the dark because daylight is short at that time of the year.

For almost 10 days, the ever-changing posse scoured the countryside surrounding the Rat River area and Johnson's cabin, until there was finally a break in the search. On Monday, January 25, almost a month after the Mad Trapper ordeal had begun, tracks matching the unique pattern of Johnson's snowshoes were spotted west, near the Richardson Mountains. Three days later, another report of Johnson's possible whereabouts was provided by a Native guide who wasn't sure if he'd heard two shots fired near the Bear River, or if it was simply the pop of a tree cracking in the intense cold. If they were gunshots, perhaps it was Johnson trying to catch some supper.

Finally, on January 30, a group of searchers led by Constable Millen came upon a stand of trees and heard a man cough. Was it Johnson? When they noticed the telltale signs of snowshoe prints, they had their answer. It was Johnson. Better still, it appeared he wasn't aware that he'd been spotted.

Anxious to get their man, and cognizant that they couldn't wait him out in the extreme cold without dire consequences, the men moved forward. One of Millen's men took a misstep, alerting Johnson to the sound of an approaching enemy. Unfazed by the intrusion, Johnson reacted quickly and with great precision, grabbing his gun and shooting. Millen and his men returned the fire, but despite their apparent advantage and the sudden silence from Johnson, the lawmen didn't emerge as victors in this exchange. After sitting Johnson out for two hours, Millen and his constables advanced toward the brush where the man had taken cover. Waiting until the exact moment when he knew he'd be able to hit his target, Johnson unleashed another round of fire. Undeterred by Johnson's aggression, Millen held his ground and fired back. Johnson fired once more. This time his bullet found its mark, and Millen fell to the ground.

Stunned by what they'd witnessed, Millen's men returned fire while Garlund dropped on his belly and slithered his way toward Millen. Once there, he tied Millen's bootlaces together, forming a crude but serviceable handle, and dragged the officer to safety.

But it was too late. Millen had likely died instantly from a bullet to the chest.

Despite the hail of gunfire into Johnson's hiding place, he escaped once again. While two of Millen's fellow officers constructed a platform on which to place their colleague's body to protect it from scavenging animals, a third officer rushed back to Aklavik to dispatch news of Millen's death.

If Johnson thought he'd get away with the attempted murder of King, and now the murder of Millen, he was mistaken. Inspector Eames had an idea that would put an end to the manhunt. It was a plan that had never been executed in the hunt for a fugitive in Canada's history. Eames asked the federal government for a surveillance aircraft to help the men on the ground to locate the outlaw. It was an expensive request—the total cost for the services of World War I flying ace Wilfred "Wop" May, mechanic Jack Bowen and a Bellanca Pacemaker monoplane was $4391.65, a staggering sum of money during the Great Depression. But Eames was convinced through his experience with the elusive, cunning and resourceful Johnson that using a plane was necessary, especially given that Johnson was headed due west. At this point in the chase, it seemed clear to Eames and other members of the force that Johnson had his sights set on Alaska, and the Mounties wouldn't get their man if he made it across the border into the U.S.

Rat River Recluse Still Eludes Authorities
Albert Johnson

Over the previous several weeks, the media had followed the story of what at that time was being hailed as one of the largest manhunts in Canada's history. Journalists dubbed Johnson the "Mad Trapper of Rat River," playing off earlier speculation that Johnson had gone crazy as a result of his self-imposed isolation. But Eames and his men knew that Johnson wasn't crazy; he was nothing more than a cold-blooded killer, and a very smart one at that. Now that a man with the celebrity of Wop May had joined in the hunt, the story gained even more momentum, and people around the world were talking about the Canadian Mounties and their elusive fugitive.

Whenever the weather made flight possible, May and Bowen surveyed the scene from the vantage point of several hundred feet in the sky and monitored the area where Mounties expected Johnson was travelling. They also dropped supplies to the men on the ground and retrieved Millen's body for transport back to Aklavik.

From February 7, when May and Bowen first arrived in the North, to February 12, frequent and persistent storms limited the amount of aerial work the men could do. So, too, was the ground search handicapped. Officers hoped Johnson's progress was being stalled as well, but that wasn't the case. Peter Alexei, another First Nations guide who was travelling in the area and noticed a strange trail, determined that the fugitive Johnson had somehow managed to scale a roughly 1525-metre summit in the Richardson Mountains, with no climbing gear and relatively few provisions, and was progressing west. Alexei knew this because he'd seen Johnson's snowshoe tracks just a couple of kilometres from La Pierre House. With this new information, it was determined that Johnson had traversed more than 137 kilometres and was already well into the Yukon. It was only a matter of time before he conquered the last leg of his journey and claimed immunity in the United States.

Eames and his men decided to establish temporary headquarters closer to their quarry. From his new control centre in La Pierre House, Eames continued to monitor his men's efforts. By now, the RCMP had been hunting Johnson for seven weeks, and everyone was getting tired. Eames knew they needed to close in soon or risk losing Johnson.

While the weather conditions proved to be a tricky deterrent in the search for the killer, the land was a little more forgiving. Although snow was falling as heavily as any other time in the hunt, the ground retained the prints left behind by Johnson's snowshoes. It was therefore easier to track the direction Johnson was moving.

Johnson, of course, was also aware of this development, and in an effort to confuse the Mounties, he wore his snowshoes backwards. He also doubled back on his tracks from time to time or wandered among a herd of caribou, using their many prints to hide his own and to confuse his pursuers. The amount of time Johnson spent trying to confuse the authorities made sense in some respects. At the same time, his actions made it look like he was toying with the Mounties, downplaying the seriousness of his situation.

The morning of February 17 was crisp and clear. With land and air crews operating in full swing, Johnson needed more than cunning to see the sunset that day; he'd need Lady Luck on his side. That was not to be.

At about noon, Royal Canadian Signals Corps Sergeant Heps Hersey was leading his dog team around a bend on the frozen Eagle River when saw Johnson. Hersey instructed the man standing just 300 metres in front of him to surrender peacefully. The request fell on deaf ears, and Johnson opened fire. Bullet shells littered the ice like dead flies in the summer as the other members of the team rushed to Hersey's aid and started shooting. Standing in the open, with no log fortress or stand of trees to use for protection, Johnson didn't have a chance. Still, he wouldn't surrender. The man crumpled to the ground, but not before seven bullets riddled his body. Finally, the 49-day manhunt had come to an end, and Johnson lay face down, dead.

The victory came with a cost, though. Sergeant Hersey was also on the ground, bleeding profusely and gasping for breath. One of Johnson's bullets had hit Hersey's knee, then ricocheted off his elbow and into the officer's chest, collapsing one of his lungs in the process. Hersey needed immediate medical attention; luckily, Wop May and his monoplane were still in the area. Officers loaded Hersey into one of the sleds and rushed him to the plane. May transported the injured officer to Aklavik, where doctors and nurses rushed to his side and tended to his wounds. Hersey survived.

The following day, May returned to the site of the final gunfight to retrieve Johnson's body and transport it to Aklavik. There, Dr. Urquhart completed a post-mortem and reported the details of Johnson's physical condition prior to his death. The man's ordeal had seriously depleted his reserves, and he'd lost at least 20 pounds in the previous seven weeks. Other than that, he appeared to be in good shape. An official inquest was held, and the RCMP were cleared of any wrongdoing in the death of Albert Johnson:

> *We, the jury, find that the man known as Albert Johnson came to his death from concentrated rifle fire from a party composed of members of the Royal Canadian Mounted Police and others, Johnson having been called upon to surrender by several members of the party and still deliberately resisted arrest, we are satisfied that no responsibility rests with any member of the party, or the party as a whole. We are further satisfied from the evidence that the party had no other means of effecting Johnson's capture except by the method employed.*

As far as the public was concerned, the case of the Mad Trapper of Rat River had come to a close. But one disturbing detail still hadn't been revealed. No one knew who the man actually was. In fact, no one knew if Albert Johnson was his real name. Who was he? Why did he have such disdain for the police? Where did he come from?

For the next several decades, law officials, scientists and journalists took part in another massive Canadian manhunt—the hunt to discover Albert Johnson's true identity.

Without personal interaction with the man who called himself Albert Johnson, any theories about who he was and where he came from were purely conjecture stemming from rare personal contacts and the seven-week chase that led to his death. Based on that alone, authorities initially developed a few opinions about the man.

Noticing that Johnson's posture was stooped over to one side, it was believed that he had worked hard most of his life, perhaps carrying heavy loads, and he was beginning to show the strain of that labour. That he stocked up on kidney pills seemed to reinforce the idea that he had been in some kind of pain.

In the six months that he lived in the Fort McPherson area, Johnson rarely spoke. When he did, people noticed he had what they thought was a slight Scandinavian accent. And although he looked like he might have come from an impoverished environment, having arrived with no gear, he had a lot of cash on his person.

Johnson presented himself as a loner, an eccentric, and a man who was perhaps developing a mental illness. And yet, the fact that he eluded an army of police officers for such a long time, burning the same amount of energy as someone who was running a marathon every day—as one expert later proposed—suggested that he was not only strong physically, but also mentally.

Clearly, the fugitive who'd acquired the moniker of "Mad Trapper" was an enigma.

In the years following Johnson's death, the RCMP looked into several possibilities when trying to learn more about the man. There was some suggestion that Johnson was really a loner named Arthur Nelson who came to the Yukon in 1927. People who'd met Nelson said he matched Johnson's description, spoke with a Scandinavian accent, was reclusive and reluctant to reveal anything about himself or his history, and he carried several weapons that were the same as those found with Johnson. Nelson also appeared to purchase a healthy supply of kidney pills. In 1931, Nelson reportedly left the Yukon, and no one really knew where he'd gone.

Was it possible that Johnson and Nelson were the same person? Or was Johnson some kind of opportunist and, coming across Nelson on his travels, had killed the man and helped himself to Nelson's supplies?

While working on a research paper in 1962, a North Dakota Minot State University student named Wallace Rustad posed the possibility that Albert Johnson might actually be a man named Johnny Johnson, a North Dakota resident who disappeared some time around 1922. Johnny reportedly had repeated run-ins with the law and landed himself in jail on several occasions. When Rustad showed a photograph of the deceased Albert Johnson to Petra Johnson, Johnny's mother, she confirmed Rustad's theory that the two men were the same person.

While Johnny's story bore some resemblance to that of the mysterious Mad Trapper, and Rustad's theory has been upheld by several other notable researchers and authors, there was still the small matter of DNA. Would Johnny Johnson's DNA match that of the elusive man of the Canadian Arctic?

※

In 2007, a forensics team organized by Michael Jorgensen and Carrie Gour of Myth Merchant Films in Spruce Grove, Alberta, set out to exhume Albert Johnson's body. This team of experts, handpicked from universities and institutions across Canada, set out to collect whatever scientific information they could after Johnson's body had been kept, undisturbed, for 75 years in the frozen ground. They wanted answers to the questions that were more elusive than the Mad Trapper himself: who was this man, and from where did he hail? After acquiring the necessary permission from Aklavik's community elders to exhume Johnson's body, a crew prepared to film the exhumation and subsequent data collection for a Discovery Channel documentary entitled *Hunt for the Mad Trapper*. The scientists involved assembled their gear and started to dig.

For hours, workers manually dug in the area identified as the spot where Albert Johnson was buried those many years ago. They even called for the assistance of a backhoe, which speeded up the process considerably until it broke and the shovels had to be pulled out once again. Radar equipment had been used to identify the site where Johnson's grave should have been, but in the end, it was Gwich'in elder Mary Kendi who pointed out the correct location of Johnson's grave. A scant metre into the ground and the sound of metal hitting old wood announced that Kendi had been right.

After Albert Johnson's remains were taken from the ground and a short ceremony held to pray for the well-being of his eternal soul, work on collecting information finally began.

The moment of truth arrived. Would what was left of Johnson's body give up any clues as to his identity? Or would the coffin contain nothing more than a skeleton, and the entire excursion prove to be a waste of valuable time and resources?

Once the coffin lid was raised, the members of the group felt a general sense of pleasant astonishment. Although what remained was primarily Johnson's skeleton, his nails, which no longer clung to fleshy fingers, were all intact inside the coffin. The infamous tufts of hair, Johnson's teeth and bits of flesh still clung to one of his thighbones. Each of these items provided investigators with helpful DNA information about the person they belonged to, and the first thing they confirmed was that the remains were indeed those of the Mad Trapper of Rat River.

It was the elaborate dental work that cemented the conclusion. The bridgework and presence of gold and silver fillings indicated that although Johnson didn't leave many possessions behind when he died, he must have come from a financially well-to-do family. Even though the dental work dated back to a few years before the Depression hit, it would have cost a considerable sum of money, and most working-class people wouldn't have been able to afford such luxury.

The surprises continued to reveal themselves in regard to Johnson's true identity. Dr. David Sweet, forensic odontologist and DNA specialist with the University of British Columbia, was charged with two tasks: to find out everything he could about Johnson through his teeth, and to pull a DNA sample from the skeleton. Sweet collected DNA from several parts of the remains and was especially successful in extracting a large portion from the marrow of one of Johnson's leg bones. Not only was Sweet able to get sufficient samples for the project, but the analysis of those specimens provided the crew with a complete genetic profile. This was a huge surprise because samples taken from human remains aren't always so forthcoming and often provide only partial identification. There was also a large amount of DNA available for comparing Johnson's genetic profile with families who suspected they might be related to him.

A new way of using the information derived from DNA analysis is in the field of geotracking. Dr. Lynne Bell, a forensic anthropologist with Simon Fraser University, has taken a keen interest in studying this method of determining what part of the world a person might have lived in during their lives. In Johnson's case, tracking his geographic movements might give investigators the edge they needed to discover where he came from and reveal more clues about the man's true identity. Bell analyzed Johnson's bones, teeth and any other available tissue, assessing data such as isotope values to collate the geographic information in Johnson's case. Her findings suggested that Johnson wasn't a Canadian but probably came from the Corn Belt of the United States, or possibly emigrated from Norway.

Along with the medical science used to paint a more accurate picture of Albert Johnson, Glenn Woods was brought in on the project. One-time director of the RCMP's Behavioural Sciences branch, Woods had clocked 35 years of experience as a psychological profiler. After being briefed on the Mad Trapper's story, Woods was asked to develop a profile of the elusive man. Woods' analysis of the case reinforced the facts derived from the physical findings. Woods, too, didn't believe Johnson was a career criminal. Instead, some kind of trigger likely pushed him into making a poor decision that caused him to seek solitude. Woods believed that Johnson was "an anal, meticulous guy" who valued his freedom above all else and likely perceived the presence of an RCMP officer at his door as a threat to that freedom. Johnson was disciplined and intelligent. He was also a "true hermit" who, if the "singing, humming and whistling" some people reported hearing when meeting up with him at various times was any indication, thoroughly preferred his own company over anyone else's.

As pieces of the puzzle continued to find their place in the jigsaw that was Albert Johnson, it was clearly time to move on to the next step in the investigation: testing DNA samples from individuals claiming to be related to him.

Edmonton author Barbara Smith was a member of the team working on the Discovery Channel documentary. In her book, *The Mad Trapper: Unearthing a Mystery*, Smith explains her role in sorting through the numerous calls from an interested public looking to find answers to their own family puzzles or perhaps provide an answer to one of Canada's most compelling mysteries. Smith rifled through the claims, determined which requests most closely fit the information collected through the team's work, and contacted individuals whose stories were plausible enough to warrant the expense of a DNA analysis.

One of the more popular claims as to the identity of the Mad Trapper was that he was Johnny Johnson, the Norwegian emigrant from North Dakota who was also discovered to be an ex-convict. The suggestion, as originally postulated by Wallace Rustad and supported through several well-researched volumes of nonfiction by author Dick North, was ruled out after Ole Getz, Johnny Johnson's great-nephew, provided a DNA sample for comparison.

Another possibility put forth by an Albertan named Mark Fremmerlid suggested that Albert Johnson was actually his great uncle, Sigvald Haaskjold, a Norwegian emigrant who struck out on his own after moving to Canada with his family, never to be heard from again. Fremmerlid was so convinced of the connection between his family and the elusive hermit of Rat River that he wrote and self-published a book about it. A DNA test ruled out that possibility.

Several other families whose stories sounded like a plausible fit to the one of Albert Johnson offered DNA samples for comparison. None of the tests proved to be a match. In the end, *The Hunt for the Mad Trapper* concluded without a definitive answer to the mystery, as did Smith's book on the topic. But the evidence unveiled throughout the process is something that can be drawn on again and again should the circumstances warrant it.

In the meantime, Albert Johnson has maintained his status as a true hermit. His body may have been recovered after one of the most documented manhunts in Canadian history, but his identity, at least, remains on the country's most wanted list.

Painted Black
THE DONNELLY FAMILY

~

*I think there were about twenty of them (that) ran
into the house.... I don't know how many came
in afterwards—I was still lying in bed when they came in,
and then I jumped out and crawled under the bed...*

–Johnny O'Connor, from donnellys.com

The woman had been working for hours stooped over in the hot July sun, tending to her family's small crops and looking over her shoulder now and again, presumably to check that her boys were focused on their chores. People in Biddulph Township spoke in low whispers whenever they saw her. The masculine-looking mother of seven wasn't a social butterfly and didn't have a string of friends to rush to her side and offer their help in the sad matter that had occurred just a month earlier, on that fateful June day in 1857. Still, no one could help but feel sorry for the woman. Pioneer women had to be strong, but how much could even a woman of her vigour be expected to handle before crumbling under the pressure?

Over the months that followed, the woman's neighbours learned just how determined and resourceful she could be. The crop was harvested in good time. The animals seemed to be thriving. It appeared that she had partially tamed her pack of unruly boys; they were always good workers, but it looked like they were putting in an almost heroic effort for their mother. She would need that kind of committed work ethic if she were to maintain the family's small farm under the circumstances.

People noticed something odd, though. With all that added work on her shoulders, with little time to prepare elaborate meals and even less time to rest, how was it then, they wondered, that at times she appeared larger than usual? Perhaps their eyes were deceiving them, but sometimes she looked as though she might have grown a few inches taller.

Of course, there were some theories about what was actually going on. At least, the people of Biddulph Township had their theories, even if the police seemed woefully disinterested.

Either way, no one was about to let on that there were times when the woman working in the Donnellys' fields was most probably a man, wearing his wife's clothing.

⁂

James Donnelly was born tough, which was a good thing. Living in County Tipperary in the province of Munster, Ireland, during a time of considerable civil and political unrest meant a man had to know how to use his fists and be willing to apply that knowledge if he had any chance at survival. By the time James belted out his first wail on March 7, 1816, his home country had been embroiled in a succession of bitter land disputes for more than a century. Landlords wielded their power over what some viewed as an inferior class with whom they begrudgingly shared their country by allowing them to cut turf or graze their livestock. The poor, downtrodden labourers could never hope to own their own piece of land, and tension between the two socioeconomic groups was worsened by the fact that the rich landowners could evict the peasants from the land they might have worked on for generations whenever the landlord wanted. After many decades of that kind of oppression, commoners like the Donnellys began to fight back.

Along with conflicts over land, there was growing hostility among Catholics and Protestants. Ireland had adopted Christianity long before war raged between the two religious factions. But as one leader after another announced that "God," as they interpreted him to be, was on their side in the battle to conquer the green isle and reign supreme, a schism was created between the two groups. When the Protestants ran the country, the families who called themselves Catholic were oppressed. When a government embracing Catholic values reigned, Protestant factions found themselves impoverished.

When James was born, a government with Protestant beliefs ruled Northern Ireland. Catholics like the Donnelly family were kept ignorant and poor; their children didn't have access to any form of education, and each family's earning power was severely restricted by limitations imposed on them, such as the legislation prohibiting them to live nearer than eight kilometres from a large centre. Because he was a Catholic, James had to learn to survive by his own cunning and grit. There was no easy road for Catholic Irish men like James and his kin. In fact, there wasn't even the remotest possibility of advancement. By the time he was old enough to make a living and raise a family, peasant farmers were no longer allowed to use the land for grazing or cutting turf. It was an impossible situation.

As Donnelly and his contemporaries saw it, the only way they could even dare to strive for something better than mere survival was to fight back with violence. Over time, the land they all loved was coloured red from the spilled blood of many a deadly battle fought by vigilante groups such as the Whiteboys, a group of men who took unjust situations into their own hands and wore white shirts over their jackets to avoid identification by their victims.

Of course, violence often begets violence, and that's exactly what happened in Northern Ireland. Rival groups such as the Blackfeet emerged, and significant factions often formed among the members when they disagreed on how to handle one problem or another and broke off into their own subgroups. This sometimes resulted in Catholics and Protestants fighting among themselves.

PAINTED BLACK
THE DONNELLY FAMILY

It was against this backdrop of violence that a young Johannah Magee (McGee) first fell in love with the strapping, young James Donnelly, who was a member of the Blackfeet. Johannah knew he was capable of holding his own in almost any situation. He was a man who knew how to take care of himself, and that was a vital quality when it came to marrying and raising a family. Like any young, Irish lass, Johannah wanted to find herself a husband, and James looked like the perfect candidate.

Johannah was born on September 22, 1820, and there were a few stories circulating about how the couple met. One suggests the two were in love but forbidden from seeing each other because Johannah's father, an important Irish judge, didn't approve of the union. Another version of their meeting has Johannah seeing James embroiled in a fistfight at the Clonmel County Fair in 1840. James easily emerged the victor, demonstrating his prowess and forever stealing the heart of his beloved Johannah.

Either way, James and Johannah married on November 8, just a few short months after they met, and promptly started their family. By 1842, the couple had welcomed their first son, James Jr., and three years later another baby, a boy they named William, joined the growing clan. Eventually, the couple had another five boys: John in 1847, Patrick in 1849, Michael in 1850, Robert in 1853 and Thomas in 1854. The Donnellys' only daughter, Jenny, was the last born, arriving in 1857.

But before William, their first Canadian-born child, entered the picture, James struck out for the New World and the chance at a better life for his growing family.

By the time James and Johannah settled into a 40-hectare parcel of land in Biddulph Township, now known as Lucan Biddulph, an incorporated township in Ontario, the family had already endured all kinds of hardship. The boat trip to Canada was a far cry from the comfortable, 45-day journey that greedy ticket agents promised to desperate immigrants looking for a more prosperous future. Once loaded onto what Peter Edwards, in his book *Night Justice: The True Story of the Black Donnellys* referred to as nothing better than a "floating coffin," passengers praying for a promising future had no better than an 80-percent chance of surviving the journey. Those who made the journey to the New World often had to endure as many as three months of being tossed about in rough seas before setting foot on dry land again. And once they stepped off the boat and onto Canadian soil, they were subjected to lengthy quarantines in conditions as deplorable as their ship ride had been before being granted a medical clearance by government officials and finally allowed to venture into their new country.

Although sources again differ, most suggest that James arrived in Canada some time in 1844, with plans to set down roots before sending for his wife and son. While he worked at several trades in London to earn enough money to send for his family,

Johannah, it appears, grew tired of waiting and made her own way to the New World sometime later that same year. One story tells how Johannah and James Jr. met up with their patriarch while walking from London to Biddulph Township—the area attracted large numbers of Irish settlers, many of them hailing from Tipperary. As chance would have it, mother and son decided to rest for a bit and noticed James Sr. working in a nearby field. Jubilant at their reunion, the small family set out to clear a patch of land in Biddulph Township and started dreaming about the farm they'd establish there one day.

Still, they needed money to build that dream, and for a time, the family lived in London as James Sr. continued to work. Most historians suggest that William was born in London in 1845, and James Sr. and Johannah were thrilled to add another son to their budding brood. Of course, the more superstitious among their acquaintances weren't so sure about the new baby. William had the misfortune of being born with a clubfoot, which many believed was a sign of the devil. Mom and Dad Donnelly, of course, scoffed at such nonsense, and young William wasn't treated any differently than his siblings.

By 1848, the Donnellys had scraped together enough cash to leave London and begin farming the piece of land they had claimed, which was roughly six kilometres from the township's largest settlement of Lucan. The farm was along an area nicknamed the "Roman Line Road" because of all the Irish Roman Catholic families who had settled there. James Sr. set out to build a farmhouse, a barn and assorted outbuildings. Looking over the lush property, Johannah was obviously pleased. "We'll call our place Greenland, and here we'll raise our family," she told James Sr. The Donnellys had struggled hard to start building toward their dream. But with stories of a devastating potato famine in their homeland and many of their friends and family in Ireland dying of starvation, the future looked like a rainbow of promise compared with what they had left behind.

They could have never imagined that the struggles of the past would pale in comparison to the difficulties that lay before them.

The events leading up to a "good day gone sour" started months before Bill Maloney's barn raising on June 27, 1857. The Donnellys were among a large number of Tipperary Irish drawn to settle in Biddulph Township. But despite the fresh start and the increasing opportunities with new alliances, petty disputes and long-standing grudges from the old country often resurfaced. The barn raising was the chance to put aside those grievances and work together to help a neighbour and build a sense of community in the process.

James Sr. arrived at the Maloney farm ready to work. Anxious to do his part and show his neighbours what a strong and capable young man he was growing into was Donnelly's second son, William. Father and son worked side by side the entire day, along with the other men of the community.

Also at the barn raising was Patrick Farrell. A relative newcomer to the community, the former blacksmith had arrived in the area to claim a parcel of land he'd leased a year earlier, only to find the Donnellys had already inhabited it.

There is considerable discrepancy about whether the Donnellys knew the land they'd squatted on and claimed as their own already belonged to someone else, or if they believed it wasn't spoken for and all their hard work earned them the right to keep it. After all, there was such a thing as squatter's rights in parts of Canada, and the family had cleared the brush, tilled the earth and raised successful crops long before anyone ever questioned their right to do so. Either way, the piece of land was indeed owned by a man named John Grace of London Township. And even though he neglected it for many years, he paid off the mortgage, and in 1855, Grace sold the southern 20 hectares to Michael Maher. When Maher discovered his resident squatters, he tried in vain to evict the Donnellys and even went as far as trying to sue the family. But nothing ever came of the proceedings, and the Donnellys carried on as before.

Having failed at claiming his property, Maher leased it out to the unsuspecting Patrick Farrell. One source tells of the day, sometime between 1855 and 1857, when Farrell sauntered up to the land he believed would soon be his new home and found the Donnelly family comfortably settled there. Farrell's temper flared. He didn't waste a moment in confronting James Sr. and wasn't worried about the cool reception the Donnelly patriarch might give him. After all, Farrell was considerably taller and broader than James Sr., and after years of hard work, he was confident in his ability to take the man down should he face that possibility.

On the other hand, the elder Donnelly didn't feel threatened by Farrell and his sharp tongue. James Sr. was more than willing to defend both his home and his family's honour. In fact, he might have welcomed the opportunity to show his sons that it was important to stand up for oneself in a competitive world. Farrell likely considered the threat of a fight as nothing but false bravado.

That day of their first meeting, Farrell was humbled in a way he'd never been humbled before. It didn't take James Sr. long to flatten the man. All Farrell could do was dust himself off and make a hasty exit.

After that first meeting and subsequent altercation, a feud between the two men simmered, erupting every once in a while in the form of various caustic confrontations. Having fought in court for the right to live on that piece of land, Farrell and Donnelly found themselves neighbours—a legal decision awarded the northern 20 hectares to Donnelly and the southern 20 hectares to Farrell. Apparently, John Grace lost any title to his 40 hectares altogether. Although the decision left the

Donnelly family with clear and legal title to a patch of land they'd dreamed about owning for so long, it was considerably less land than they'd planned on farming. With a brood of seven boys, the loss of 20 hectares caused James Sr. and Johannah significant concern.

Donnelly and Farrell learned to share the 40 hectares known as Government Lot #18, and each built his own corner into a working farm, but whenever they came within sight of the other, they exchanged piercing glares of intense hatred. James Sr. felt as though his neighbour had stolen half of his land; Farrell believed the same was true of Donnelly. On one occasion, James Sr. was accused of firing a musket in Farrell's direction. And when Farrell found three of his cows poisoned and his barn burned to the ground, he believed it was Donnelly, or one of his rambunctious sons, who was responsible.

It's quite possible that Maloney's barn raising was the first time the two men found themselves in such close quarters since the altercation at the Donnelly homestead and the subsequent court case. Still, they were there to help a fellow neighbour build his barn, not to settle unfinished business.

To make the day move along smoothly, an ample supply of liquor was available, which most of the men drank. The booze seemed to do more than fuel Patrick Farrell with energy; it unleashed a year's worth of pent-up fury. While the group of men were focused on erecting walls and lifting rafters, Farrell supplied a running commentary of his contempt for James Sr.

Farrell's vitriolic assault didn't appear to have much effect on the elder Donnelly. Although Donnelly had proved on several occasions that he wasn't opposed to a good fight, he was focused on the job at hand. Indeed, if all that has been written about James Sr. over the intervening years since his death is true, he was remarkably composed that day.

Still, a time comes when even the most controlled individual gives way to pressure, and when Farrell rushed at James Sr. with an axe, Donnelly responded with his fists, managing to knock the man to the ground in the process. A brawl ensued, and at some point in the altercation, Farrell reached for a handspike and lashed out in James' direction. Donnelly also grabbed a handspike. His thrust met Farrell's left temple, and his opponent fell to the ground one final time.

James Sr. had won this battle, but it would cost him dearly.

According to stories that appeared in the *London Free Press* after the deadly fight at Maloney's barn raising, Donnelly was well within his rights to defend himself against the verbal-turned-physical attack hurled at him by Farrell. It was Farrell, witnesses agreed, who threw the first punch, and Farrell who first tried to use a handspike against his opponent.

Donnelly, on the other hand, seemed overwhelmed by the reality that he had killed a man, and he simply disappeared. That decision could have fuelled doubt among residents who had previously supported Donnelly's actions. By not turning himself in to the authorities and providing his version of events, James Sr. became a wanted man.

For more than a year, no one spoke to or saw the patriarch of the Donnelly clan. At least, no one admitted to seeing him. In time, though, a few of Biddulph's residents started to piece things together. Johannah, for example, seemed to be managing extremely well under the circumstances. In fact, she managed to run the farm as well on her own as James Sr. had when he was home. Neighbours routinely saw her tending to the fields. There were times when Johannah's typically solid and masculine body seemed to have grown in stature, but the difference was so slight that it was hard to be sure. Still, people were starting to talk among themselves. Was it possible that James Sr. hadn't left the area at all and was actually working the fields with his wife and wearing her dresses to throw off any suspicion?

The answer to that question became increasingly obvious as the months passed and Johannah's belly expanded with what was obviously another child. If James Sr. was hiding out somewhere, he must have made a few forays home. Regardless of the evidence, no one reported their suspicions to the authorities. Even with what seemed like proof that James Sr. was in the area, residents were reluctant to inform the police. After all, no one wanted to be labelled a snitch. Justice, if necessary, was better doled out among neighbours. And at that point, no one really blamed James Sr. for having killed Farrell.

Baby Jennie was born that winter of 1857 when James Sr. was on the run. It was a difficult and bitter season, and although there were rumours that he sometimes returned to the homestead to seek refuge from the cold, Donnelly knew that he couldn't spend another winter on the lam. In May 1858, the family's patriarch finally turned himself in. Some sources suggest he did so under the advice of a family friend, Mitchell Haskett. Haskett was sympathetic to James' plight and believed that although Donnelly wouldn't get off without some punishment, he couldn't imagine him receiving a stiff sentence.

Haskett couldn't have been more mistaken. Not long after James Sr. turned himself in, a trial was held in the Goderich County courthouse. Despite several witnesses repeating their stories about Farrell's aggressive actions and Donnelly's defensive reactions, James Sr. received the harshest punishment possible. One of the country's most wanted men at the time was found guilty of murder and sentenced to death by hanging.

The tough-as-nails Johannah crumpled from the shock.

Nobody saw it coming. To be sure, James Sr. was a strong man who could turn dangerous if pushed, but a hangman's noose? Even folks who weren't fond of the Donnellys were surprised at the verdict. After all, an incident earlier that same year resulted in a premeditated revenge killing, and the perpetrators in that case spent five years defending their actions in court.

In the end, they were let off with a stern reprimand and instructions to lead an exemplary life and stay out of trouble. Certainly the situation at the barn raising was unfortunate and a man was dead, but James Sr.'s actions could not compare with a premeditated revenge killing.

After James Sr. was sentenced, Johannah got to work. Not one to give up in the face of a challenge, she approached Big Jim Hodgins. The Tipperary man had founded Biddulph Township; it was Hodgins' visits back to the old country and his stories of lush farmland and the possibilities for a bright future in Canada that had attracted the Donnellys to the area in the first place. Johannah asked Hodgins to draw up a petition for clemency in her husband's case, and for weeks, she and her children attended Sunday services at various churches throughout Lucan, sharing their story and asking for signatures. She also spent hours walking the streets of the community, approaching anyone she might have missed and asking for their support.

Her persistence paid off when her petition made its way to John A. Macdonald, the attorney general of Canada at the time. Reviewing the petition, Macdonald noticed that Donnelly received support from both Catholic and Protestant residents, and many of the names appeared to belong to prominent citizens. It might have occurred to the politician that supporting such a cause when an election was on the horizon might buy him a few votes. And so it was that Macdonald commuted James' sentence from the death penalty to 10 years in the Kingston penitentiary; James would be released in seven years for good behaviour.

Johannah had succeeded in conquering her first mountainous challenge. Now she had to plan exactly how she'd maintain the family farm and raise seven sons and a daughter in the process. Legend has it that Johannah held a family meeting, assigned various tasks to each of her children, explained the importance of the family working together, and then she did something most mothers wouldn't do—she told them to learn how to fight. They were to scrap among themselves if necessary. And as James Sr. served his time in jail and was being hardened with threats of lashes or body restraints or being locked away in an upright box the size of a coffin for offences as minor as smiling or speaking French, his boys were being strengthened under the tutelage of their mother's stern guidance.

On a fine fall day in 1865, James Sr. was finally released from prison, and with great anticipation, Johannah and the clan met the stagecoach carrying their long-absent patriarch.

"It's sivin devils I've raised for ye, Jim, an' this here's young Jinny," Johannah said as she welcomed her husband home. Many a family in Biddulph Township and nearby Lucan would have agreed with Johannah's assessment of her boys.

During Donnelly's seven-year absence, his seven sons allegedly rained terror throughout the area. Over the years, folks reported that items like tools or farm equipment had gone missing from their property. On occasion, barns or homes were burned to the ground, and although no one could prove it, the fires often coincided with a spat between the owner of the property and one of the Donnellys. Reports of animal mutilation surfaced from time to time; again, some residents cast suspicion on the Donnelly boys for these horrific deeds, while others argued that the family had far too much respect for animals to commit such heinous acts. The Donnellys certainly weren't responsible for every act of vandalism or theft, but the boys often had a hand in some of the complaints, earning them a reputation that most mothers don't want for their children.

Johannah, of course, was proud of her boys, and woe to the person who dared to criticize her youngsters. The Donnellys clearly had allies in their community, which was evident when several families helped Johannah make payment on a loan that had fallen into arrears, thus assisting her in maintaining the family farm during her husband's incarceration. But many folks despised the Donnelly children, and they were often taunted and teased by their peers. As far as Johannah was concerned, her boys needed to be as tough as their father.

Life at that time in Biddulph Township's history mirrored that of many new settlements in the western world. Petty quarrels sometimes erupted into deadly brawls, competitions between businesses occasionally turned ugly, and vandalism and theft were facts of life. While communities usually boasted a lawman or two on the payroll, residents often doled out their own form of justice from time to time, especially when they felt that the law wasn't doing its job. And vigilante justice was something the Donnelly boys were well known for.

Perhaps it was the sheer number of sons that Johannah had birthed and their talent at fending for themselves no matter what it took and against the mildest of slights that drew such disdain from some of their neighbours. Whatever the case, people generally went out of their way to steer clear of the boys and avoid any chance of offending them.

To add to the rough edges the Donnelly boys all too often flaunted, they weren't overly particular about what they viewed as trivial matters, such as marrying outside the Catholic faith. Given that hurts still smouldered over the conflict-ridden, old-country history between Protestants and Catholics, it didn't bode well when several of the boys married Protestant women. And although Will married a woman named Norah Kennedy from his own Catholic parish, the girl's brother, Big Jack, or "the Bull," as Will often referred to him, was vehemently against the union. The opposition coming from Norah's family was strange considering that at one time Will and her brothers had been good friends. It appeared that even in circumstances that should have been opportunities to celebrate, friction had a way of following the Donnelly boys.

That friction was about to explode.

Not all of the Donnelly boys were interested in farming. In 1870, Will and Michael started driving stagecoaches for the McPhee and Keefe line. It was a competitive field with too many stagecoach companies vying for limited customers, but never ones to be dissuaded by competition, Will and Michael purchased the line on May 23, 1873. Bob and Tom started driving for their brothers, making it truly a family-run business.

The business venture may have come as a surprise to some who knew the Donnelly boys, but they were always courteous to their fares and conducted themselves like the gentlemen their mother had always believed they were. Still, this was only the first step to remaining competitive. Stagecoach operators from every company pushed their animals and rigs as hard as possible to earn the right to brag that they offered the fastest and safest service. When that wasn't enough to draw more customers, owners were often accused of resorting to more destructive measures, such as damaging equipment or starting fires, to combat their competition.

Pat Flanagan was one of the Donnellys' stiffest competitors, and wild stories of how one or the other had stolen a customer or vandalized their competitor's equipment in the hope of pushing their nemesis out of business were common. At one point, Flanagan's stables were set ablaze. Another time, his stagecoach was literally sawed into pieces and his horses brutally mutilated. Although no one could ever prove who was responsible for these and many other incidents, fingers frequently pointed in the direction of the Donnelly clan. After all, who else would stoop to such low levels to better their own situation? Still, the Donnellys' stagecoach line was gaining a name for its reliable service, despite the young men's reputation for causing chaos.

In January 1879, another newcomer of note in Biddulph Township was Father John Connolly. The 50-year-old priest was taking over St. Patrick's Church in Lucan and was looking forward to getting to know his new flock. Connolly, a man of considerable education and culture, was replacing Father Girard, a kind and gentle soul who found his neighbours too unruly to control. Girard knew of the infighting between his parishioners and others, and he could often smooth things over with love and patience.

Father Connolly took a different approach with his flock. During his sermons, he routinely referred to what he considered grievous situations in the community and chastised those who might have been involved. Frequently, at least as far as William was concerned, the new man of the cloth seemed somewhat skewed in his thinking, prejudiced even, and pointed to members of the Donnelly family as the perpetrators in many of those cases. On several occasions, a Donnelly hadn't actually been involved or wasn't anywhere near an event that Connolly spoke of, but public opinion against the family grew. Even their one-time friends thought twice about maintaining a relationship with them. After all, James Sr. was once a wanted man and had served time for murder, and several of his sons had spent time in jail for various and sundry less-serious charges. The general consensus was that if the community wanted to squelch its reputation as being one of the wildest towns in the new country, it had to deal with the Donnelly clan. Father Connolly had an idea for how to do just that.

On June 15, 1879, Father Connolly once again addressed his flock from the authority of his pulpit. He told his congregation of his plans to establish a "property protection association," and that he expected his parishioners to pledge their allegiance to this organization. Whenever there was a theft in the community, all the families who'd joined the association would agree to have their property searched. They further agreed to "assist the clergyman in every way to put a stop to the depredations which are becoming a scandal to the parish," suggesting, some might have thought, that the Donnellys might have threatened the good Father. Anyone who wasn't a member of this watchdog alliance was accused by Father Connolly of being "backsliders and sympathizers of the gang which is the cause of the depredations in this community." He went on to suggest the opposing "gang" was led by none other than Will Donnelly, "that devil of a cripple."

And so it was that the foundation for Lucan's vigilance committee was laid. Perhaps it was not what Father Connolly had intended, but it was the beginning of the end of the Donnelly family.

William did not become a member of the new society, and he urged his father to rethink his initial desire to join. He also sensed that the committee was potentially dangerous, especially since it appeared that Father Connolly was picking and choosing the facts of any criminal activity as he saw fit and continually blaming the Donnellys, even with evidence to the contrary.

In a letter to the bishop, Will begged for an intervention in this matter. He bluntly stated that he believed Father Connolly was "prejudiced against [his] family," that he'd be happy to address the Father's concerns in the bishop's presence, "…and if I am wrong in this matter I will lower myself lower than the worm who crawls." Will was genuinely concerned for the safety of his family. He ended his letter with a plea: "Without meaning to show disrespect to your Lordship in any way, I beg of you, for God and in Justice, to do something about the disbanding of this society formed against us, for if something is not done I am sure it will end in bloodshed."

William Thompson had no love for the Donnellys. His distaste for the family mushroomed further when his teenaged sister, Maggie, developed an affection for Will. Thompson and his father managed to put an end to the romance despite Will's best efforts to whisk young Maggie away and make her his wife. So when Thompson discovered one of his cows missing, he naturally blamed the Donnellys.

Angry beyond reason, Thompson marched into Lucan and stirred up members of the vigilance committee, which was evolving into a kind of enforcer presence in the town. Thompson bemoaned the loss of his cow and blamed the Donnellys. Gathering the support of almost 40 men, including Will's brother-in-law, Jack Kennedy, Thompson marched to the Donnelly homestead.

Thompson accused James Sr. and Johannah, saying that they, or perhaps John or Thomas, the only two sons still living at home, had stolen his cow. James Sr. challenged Thompson, telling him to look through his fields and his barns and see for himself that he was mistaken. Thompson and his supporters did just that, and when they couldn't find a cow at the original homestead, they made their way to Will's farm.

Having been warned of the men's imminent arrival by Johannah, who tore across the fields to her son's home, Will was ready. After surveying the crowd of men gathered in his front yard, Will went back into the house, emerged with his violin and began playing "Boney Crossing the Alps." The irony of his choice in music, which was a song about Napoleon Bonaparte, wasn't lost on the members of the society who'd just participated in a "march" of their own. Eventually, the crowd dwindled. Ironically, the missing cow had never really gone missing in the first place and was discovered in a far corner of the farmer's field.

It appeared that the vigilance committee had to step back and wait for another opportunity to take down the clan. The next, best opportunity to accuse one or more of the Donnellys with a crime occurred when a neighbour's barn burned to the ground on January 15, 1880. The Ryders were once good friends with the Donnellys with, perhaps, the exception of one of the boys named Patrick, who also went by the moniker "Grouchy." But the two families quarrelled after one of the Ryders' horses had its tail shaved and had some type of election message posted on its rump. For some inexplicable reason, the Ryders believed that the Donnellys were responsible for the nasty act. Although Will refused to believe ill of the Ryders, it was soon clear that the Donnellys' friends had switched camps. Blaming the Donnellys for their incinerated barn was just the first nail in the coffin.

James Carroll was the newly appointed constable in town, which didn't bode well for the Donnellys because he and various members of the Carroll family nursed ongoing disputes with the notorious family. Carroll acquired arrest warrants for James Sr. and Johannah, who were being blamed for the barn fire at the Ryder farm. Although the evidence against the aging couple appeared nonexistent, and at the time of their arrest no witnesses came forward, they were ordered to stand trial. By now, the ongoing stress was beginning to tell on Johannah. She'd already buried two of her sons: James Jr. died in May 1877, and Michael was killed in a bar room brawl, and his funeral was held on December 12, 1879, a little over a month before this newest fiasco had begun.

On January 27, the Donnelly's niece, Bridget, who was visiting from Ireland, and Bridget O'Connor, a family friend, both testified in court that the couple was in bed, sleeping, when the fire broke out. Still, Carroll was afforded more time to dig up some kind of evidence that Johannah and James Sr. were guilty of the crime. Carroll had one more chance to prove the Donnellys' guilt before the couple's final court date of February 4.

The idea that the Donnellys might get away with being convicted of a crime, even though the general consensus was that they really weren't guilty in the first place, concerned the members of the vigilance committee. Will was tired of seeing his family repeatedly harassed by an organization that was clearly out to destroy them. The rumours circulating around Lucan suggested that if James Sr. and Johannah were found not guilty, Will planned to charge members of the society with false arrest and take them to court.

That was a event the society members were not about to let happen.

On the evening of February 3, 1880, members of the vigilance committee were preparing to put their plan into action. Gulping down several rounds of rotgut whiskey, the throng of 40 men was more than pumped for what was about to happen. Shortly after midnight on February 4, the men mounted their horses, and led by none other than Constable Carroll, made their way to the Donnelly farm.

Once they arrived, Carroll went to the back of the house while the other men stood guard in the front. Carroll knew that James Sr. never locked the back door; he also knew that there were weapons in the house, and if his plan for the evening were to succeed, he needed to ensure that he had the upper hand from the start.

While the Donnelly family slept, Carroll slipped into Tom's bedroom and clasped iron handcuffs onto the boy's wrists. The sound of Constable Carroll's whistling soon roused Johannah and Bridget, but it wasn't until Carroll was standing at James Sr.'s bedroom door that the family patriarch finally woke up.

Initially, the family assumed they were being confronted with another set of bogus charges. Indeed, that's exactly what Carroll suggested when everyone gathered in the family's living room. But he never read out the charges. Moments later, a mob of angry vigilantes burst through the front door, carrying guns, axes and anything else they could grab, wielding their weapons at the Donnellys. Anyone who'd ever held a grudge against the family was in the room, along with an assortment of old friends whose opinion about James Sr. and his kin had soured over the years. The massacre had begun.

James Sr. fell to the ground as someone hit Tom on the head with a spade. Still handcuffed, the young man was powerless to defend himself and tried to escape the carnage by rushing outside, only to be greeted by more of the mob. One knocked him to the frozen ground while Tom Ryder thrust his pitchfork into the young man. Blood poured from Tom's body, but the brutality of the night had only begun. Johannah also tried to escape through the front door, but the angry horde clubbed her and dragged her back into the house before the final blows were thrust, and she fell to the floor for the last time.

Bridget, a beautiful young woman whose only crime was that she chose the wrong time to visit her aunt and uncle, had rushed upstairs to hide as soon as she realized the men who'd come calling that night weren't interested in a peaceful arrest. Once James Sr., Johannah and Tom had been killed, one of the men remembered that Bridget was somewhere on the premises. The last thing the vigilante group wanted to do was leave a witness to their heinous actions, so they searched the property until they found their next terrified victim. After they killed Bridget, they torched the farmhouse, thinking that no one would ever be the wiser about what had actually happened that night at the Donnelly homestead.

They couldn't have been more mistaken.

Visiting the Donnellys that night was 13-year-old Johnny O'Connor. The lad had been hired to care for the family's livestock while they travelled to their scheduled court case the following day. Young Johnny had been sharing a bed with James Sr., the only bed large enough to accommodate an extra visitor, and when Constable Carroll charged James' bedroom and called for him to come out, no one had seen Johnny because he was against the wall hiding behind James Sr.'s body. Once the boy realized that the men had murder on their minds, he hid behind a clothesbasket under the bed. He showed incredible restraint by not uttering a sound or moving a muscle, even after the bed above him was drenched with coal oil and set on fire. Finally, he crept out when he no longer heard the yelps and wails of the wild men, who were now on their way to their next victim—Will Donnelly.

Some of the men leading the pack to Will's house included his brother-in-law, Big Jack Kennedy Jr.; one of the Ryder boys, a long-time friend of Will's; and Martin McLaughlin, a justice of the peace and school board representative who farmed near Will—all people the young Donnelly trusted. It was McLaughlin who knocked on Will's door and yelled, "Fire!" With several guns aimed at Will's front door, the mob just had to wait until he opened it, and Lucan's biggest nemesis, in their eyes, would be history.

As it turned out, John Donnelly answered the door, not Will. Will's younger brother was visiting that evening and responded to the ruckus outside before Will did, sealing John's fate as the final Donnelly to die that night. The mob left, thinking they'd killed Will after peppering John's body full of holes. Peering through a nearby window, Will recognized several of the attackers, many of whom he'd once called his friends, and all of them he called his neighbours. Norah woke to the commotion, was overwhelmed at what had happened and sprinkled holy water on the body of her dying brother-in-law. Will spared his pregnant wife the news that her brother had been in on the attack. Will and Norah, along with Martin Hogan, another friend who'd been visiting the evening before, spent the night clinging to each other for support through the terrifying hours before sunrise.

By morning, Will hoped he would have gathered himself together enough to set the wheels in motion to ensure the men responsible for John's death were brought to justice. He was a desperate man drowning in grief over the loss of his brother. He had yet to discover just how tragic the situation was.

⁂

Johnny O'Connor reported to the authorities what he'd seen on the night of the murders. His story, as unbelievable as it sounded, reinforced Will's report of what had happened at his own farm. There was physical evidence, names named, arrest warrants filed, people charged and court cases heard. Perhaps even more unbelievable than the massacre itself was the fact that nothing came of the charges—no one was ever found guilty of the crimes.

One legend surrounding the Donnelly family massacre revolves around the sad story of Will and his first love, Maggie. Various stories have the young woman married off by her father to an old man to keep her from Will. Another says that he hid her away until Will gave up trying to find her, and the beautiful girl became an old and lonely spinster. Every year, on the anniversary of the massacre, it was believed that Maggie hand delivered a letter to the local newspaper editor, begging for justice for the man she had once loved and his murdered kin.

In his book, *In Search of the Donnellys*, Ray Fazakas shares another story about how one of Will's brothers coped with the tragedy. Patrick's descendents tell of how their patriarch would insist his children write letters or cards to every member of the gang he believed was responsible for his family's tragedy as each anniversary of the massacre approached. Clearly, no matter how challenging the Donnelly family could be, they hadn't deserved to be butchered in such a barbaric and cruel fashion, especially young Bridget, who by all accounts was a lovely, pure young woman without a malicious bone in her body.

What will forever be a blight on Canada's legal history is that the Donnelly family was never vindicated. Their murderers will never be brought to justice.

Notes on Sources

Information for stories throughout this text was retrieved from numerous sources, including several community news outlets, online and print publications, TV news programs and special interest groups.

Media Sources

America's Most Wanted

Associated Press

Australia Securities & Investments Commission

Black Press

British Columbia Securities Commission

British Columbia Review Board

The Buffalo News

Bukisz.com

The Cairns Post

Canadian Press

CanLii

CanWest News Service

CBC News

CNN

CTV News

Explorenorth.com

FBI

Federal Bureau of Prisons

Fifth Estate

Forensic Psychiatric Institute in Port Coquitlam, BC

FOX News

Globe and Mail

GoDutch.com

Hamilton Spectator

HighBeam Research

InvestorDaily

Kamloops Daily News

Kamloops Radio NL

Kingston Whig-Standard

La Presse

Mississauga.com

Moneymanagement.com

Montreal Gazette

National Post

Northwest Territories & Yukon Radio System History Project

Northern Sentinel

The Official Donnelly Home Page

The Official Website of CRCNA Ministries

Ottawa Citizen

Priests for Life Canada

Prince of Wales Northern Heritage Centre

Pro Choice Action Network

The Province

TheRecord.com

Red Deer City RCMP Stats Archives

Reformed Online

Reuters News Agency

Star Phoenix

Sun Media Newspapers

Toronto Star

Vancouver Sun

Wikipedia

Print Sources

Anderson, Frank W., *Death of Albert Johnson*, Frontier Series, Book No. 16., Surrey, BC: Frontier Publishing Ltd., 1968, and Heritage House Publishing Company Ltd., 1980.

Edwards, Peter. *Night Justice, The True Story of the Black Donnellys*. Toronto, ON: Key Porter Books, 2004.

Hebert-Germain, Georges, *Monica la Mitraille*. Montréal, QC: Libre Expression (Free Expression—A company of Québecor Media), 1997.

Hélèna Katz, *The Mad Trapper*, Canmore, AB: Altitude Publishing Canada Ltd., 2004.

Hendley, Nate. *The Black Donnellys, The Outrageous Tale of Canada's Deadliest Feud.* Canmore, AB: Altitude Publishing Ltd., 2004.

MacIntyre, Linden, and Theresa Burke, *Who Killed Ty Conn?* Toronto, ON: Viking Canada (AHC), 2000.

North, Dick. *The Mad Trapper of Rat River: A True Story of Canada's Biggest Manhunt.* Guilford, CT: First Lyons Press, 2003.

Smith, Barbara. *The Mad Trapper: Unearthing a Mystery.* Surrey, BC: Heritage House Publishing Company Ltd., 2009.

van der Heide, A.A., *The Windmill Herald,* Vanderheide Publishing Co. Ltd.

Lisa Wojna

Bestselling author Lisa Wojna has at least 25 non-fiction books to her credit, including three others with Quagmire Press: *Canadian Con Artists, Missing! The Disappeared, Lost or Abducted in Canada* and *Unsolved Murders of Canada*. She has worked in the community newspaper industry as a writer and journalist and has travelled all over Canada from the windy prairies of Manitoba to northern British Columbia and even to the wilds of Africa. Although writing and photography have been a central part of her life for as long as she can remember, it's the people behind every story that are her motivation and give her the most fulfilment.